# PR Idea Book

## 50 Proven Tools That Really Work

Jeff Winke

Outskirts Press, Inc.
Denver, Colorado

The opinions expressed in this manuscript are solely the opinions of the author and do not represent the opinions or thoughts of the publisher. The author represents and warrants that s/he either owns or has the legal right to publish all material in this book. If you believe this to be incorrect, contact the publisher through its website at www.outskirtspress.com.

PR Idea Book
50 Proven Tools That Really Work
All Rights Reserved
Copyright © 2006 Jeff Winke
Cover Image © 2006 Ben Newby
All Rights Reserved. Used With Permission.

This book may not be reproduced, transmitted, or stored in whole or in part by any means, including graphic, electronic, or mechanical without the express written consent of the publisher except in the case of brief quotations embodied in critical articles and reviews.

Outskirts Press
http://www.outskirtspress.com

ISBN-10: 1-59800-317-8
ISBN-13: 978-1-59800-317-8

Outskirts Press and the "OP" logo are trademarks belonging to
Outskirts Press, Inc.

Printed in the United States of America

*It requires a very unusual mind to undertake the analysis of the obvious*

- Alfred North Whitehead

# Acknowledgements

Special thanks to my friend and colleague, Mike Starling, who provided valuable editing and moral support throughout the writing of this book. And of course, tremendous thanks goes to my patient wife, Carol Winke, who tolerated many "I'm getting a quick cup of coffee with Mike" four-hour absences while the book concept was being formulated and the final copy being polished.

Professionally, there have been countless mentors, sounding boards and gentle critics who have helped me. Among the many, I wish to thank Dick Yake, David Heide, John Luecke, John Hoff, Jerry Houfek, Jon Martin, John Platta, Dennis Madigan, Ken Artis, John Koski, Michael Diedrick, Kim Schnaderbeck, Pete Kennedy, Matt Wisla, Tim O'Brien, Warren Eulgen, Catherine Mansfield and others who I've regrettably missed.

Additionally, this book would not have been written without two annual week-long writing retreats I took deep in the cedar woods of Wisconsin's Door County at the South Nest Artists and Writers Center in Bailey's Harbor. Thank you Nancy Rafal and Michael Farmer for providing me with an exceptional place to write.

# Preface

This is a sourcebook – a collection of ideas, strategies and tactics that have been forged through actual use with businesses of all sizes. Operations ranged from entrepreneurially-sparked, start-up operations with spectacular better-mouse-trap ideas to Fortune® 100 mega-successes that have remained fresh, alert and agile in a marketplace where they are the target of aggressive competitors.

During a 20+ year span, I have been privileged to work in a wide variety of business-to-business markets. I have been on the inside as a paid employee and on the outside as a paid counselor. For a half-dozen year stretch, I even ran my own marketing communications firm.

I cut my PR professional teeth as a communications writer for Snap-on Tools where I was the editor of a worldwide distributed employee magazine and contributor to the company's annual report. I then worked in the mortgage insurance industry producing newsletters, training materials and marketing pieces.

Where I truly earned my "journeyman's papers" in PR was with a series of b-to-b marketing communications firms. These ad agencies exposed me to a variety of client companies ranging from manufacturers of sub-miniature plastic valves used in high-end processing to heavy-equipment manufacturers who build mining trucks with massive hauling beds large enough to easily park eight pickups.

As a PR counselor working in ad agency settings, I have worked with businesses offering professional services that ranged from toxicological laboratory services to full-line commercial and personal insurance to transportation logistics. Clients of mine have been involved in material handling, machining/metal-forming, pharmaceutical and specialty chemical processing, construction, sensors and controls, and building environment management. I have helped a bank open new branches, a large holding company change its name and a community-based dumpster manufacturer increase its sales.

The business-to-business market is a completely different animal than the consumer market. Don't let anyone tell you differently. In my estimation, the business-to-business market is far more challenging and exciting than the consumer market. Hands down it is tough. It requires more creativity on the part of management, marketing, sales and public relations to succeed.

The 50 ideas in this book are action-based tactics designed to increase sales and solidify a company's image in its marketplace. They work whether your company is a start-up concerned with creating and solidifying a consistent corporate image or an established firm maintaining its presence while underscoring the innovation that built the business and continues to fuel its growth.

The audience for this book includes everyone from the small business owner that cannot afford to hire outside counsel to the experienced practitioner looking for new ideas. This book does not explain how to put a PR plan together. There are other sources for that. This book is filled with the zap, ping, kapow that gives your PR plan the oomph to succeed.

The 50 proven tools that work are arranged in alphabetical order. They are each labeled as plainly and descriptively as possible to make it easy to find them when referring back to them at a later date.

# Table of Contents

| | |
|---|---|
| First, Some Basics | 1 |
| 1. Activity Updates | 11 |
| 2. Advertorials | 15 |
| 3. Application Reports | 19 |
| 4. Article Reprints | 23 |
| 5. Breakthrough New Product / Service Announcement | 27 |
| 6. Business Letter | 31 |
| 7. Case History/Application Story | 33 |
| 8. Cause-Related Promotions | 37 |
| 9. CD Press Kit | 39 |
| 10. Clipping/Monitoring Reports | 43 |
| 11. Community Relations | 47 |
| 12. Company Backgrounder | 49 |
| 13. Company Expert Interviews | 51 |

| | |
|---|---|
| 14. Company History | 53 |
| 15. Company Resume | 57 |
| 16. Count-down Articles | 61 |
| 17. Create Positive Publicity Opportunities | 63 |
| 18. Customer Brief | 65 |
| 19. Editor Visits | 67 |
| 20. Editorial Calendar Opportunities Matrix | 69 |
| 21. Event Sponsorships | 73 |
| 22. Expert Interview Series | 77 |
| 23. Expert Visitors | 79 |
| 24. Fact Sheet | 81 |
| 25. FAQs | 83 |
| 26. Guest Opinion Editorial | 85 |
| 27. How-to Articles | 87 |
| 28. Inquiry Management | 89 |
| 29. Jargon Dictionary | 93 |
| 30. Management Bios | 95 |
| 31. Marketplace Studies | 97 |
| 32. Market-Specific PR | 101 |
| 33. Media Day Event | 105 |
| 34. Media List Development | 109 |
| 35. Newsletter / e-Newsletter | 113 |
| 36. Online Press Room | 119 |
| 37. Press Conferences | 121 |
| 38. Press Kit | 125 |
| 39. Press Release | 131 |
| 40. Radio Presentations / Interviews | 137 |
| 41. Speaker Program | 141 |
| 42. Special Events | 143 |

| | |
|---|---|
| 43. Standing Graphs | 147 |
| 44. Syndicated Column | 151 |
| 45. Technical Articles | 153 |
| 46. Technical Brief / Profile | 155 |
| 47. Trade Show PR Efforts | 157 |
| 48. Video News Release | 169 |
| 49. Web Monitoring and Posting | 173 |
| 50. White Paper | 175 |
| Where Next? | 177 |

# First, Some Basics

Before we launch into the 50 proven tools that work, let's review a few b-to-b public relations basics.

Public relations is the planned effort to influence opinions and bring about a desired action.

So what opinions are we trying to influence? Certainly that your company should be a buyer's number one choice; that it offers the best products and/or services; that it is easy to work with; or any other powerful messages that distinguish your company from its competition in the eyes of your customers and prospects.

And what's the desired action? To get them to buy

your products or services!

A number of years ago a small manufacturing company called me for a quote on an advertising program. They had a new, innovative product they felt would open new markets and push their company to the next growth level.

When I met them, their excitement was infectious. They clearly had a unique product and the energy to push it out in the market. They also had copies of the three leading trade magazines in their market. They asked: "What will it cost to create an ad and run them in these magazines?" We set up a second meeting.

A week later, I returned with an advertising campaign that would accomplish their goals. For a quarter of the ad program costs, I suggested we implement a public relations campaign that involved:

- developing a media list,
- a contact strategy that included a press release,
- a company backgrounder to position the company in its market,
- a glamour photo of the new product, and
- a professionally-rendered illustration of an engineering schematic that showed how the product worked.

Additionally, I recommended that we visit the technical editor with the leading publication and offer him an exclusive opportunity to profile the new product. This would be followed by contact with the remaining publications. Five other key publications would be contacted by phone with the packet of material forwarded to them as follow-up. Another 47 publications on the complete media list I had developed would receive a letter expressing interest in working with them as a technical resource on any future pertinent articles they may be developing. The backgrounder was included with the letter. The new product press release, photo and illustration were sent a week later.

The company agreed to the public relations option. The technical editor of the leading publication did jump at the opportunity for the exclusive story. Each of the five key publications ran a prominent full-color new product announcement and nearly half of the 47 other publications ran the release in their new products section. Paid advertising did become important to this company's marketing efforts, but we were able to use it strategically to maintain interest in the product after our PR campaign had run its course.

This is a textbook example of the powerful and lasting impact of what I call the "C's" of public relations.

## PR is Complementary

First, public relations is *complementary* – meaning that it dovetails and works synergistically with your company's other marketing efforts. A good PR message:

- enhances or extends a paid advertising message.
- shows or demonstrates how a product is used. In other words, you might make a claim with advertising; and you can justify the claim through PR.
- reinforces your other marketing messages by adding another layer through a different channel to the message

## PR is Cost-Effective

Second, public relations is *cost-effective*. Notice I didn't say "free" – though it is true you don't pay to get something in a publication, there still are investment costs, just as you have in any kind of marketing.

Still, compared to the costs for producing an advertisement and paying for the space, it is less expensive to develop, let's say, a PR article for publication. The cost-effective value of PR is why it is used in cases where budgets are tight.

If you need to reach a lot of vertical audiences or even

just a lot of media sources within one market, PR is the money-pinching best choice. Add the fact that published results can be further merchandised by producing reprints that can be used as sales leave-behinds, in direct mail or at trade shows as handouts, and it becomes clear how a modest investment can be strategically amortized.

## PR is Credible

Third, public relations is *credible*. Anything published in the media undergoes the scrutiny of an editor and/or publisher. Thus it carries, in the mind of the reader, the implied endorsement of a respected third party. Additionally, if the piece is a case history, you have the testimonial of a satisfied customer who is on record saying your product works well.

The general consensus of the experts is that PR is at least twice as credible as advertising. Some have said it's more like three or four times more credible. You can safely take the ad space equivalent cost of space you've earned through your PR efforts and double the amount to show your doubting accountant, should there be any objections from your calculator curmudgeon.

## The Final C's

And finally, in order for PR to work, you need *constancy, consistency,* and *continuity* – in other words, you need to keep at it. In a sense, PR is just like selling – if you don't build a relationship with the press, it's a tougher sales job. Plans and programs are created for the very reason of ensuring continual contact with the media. What you're hoping to do through a planned approach is take advantage of the *cumulative* effect of your on-going efforts.

**What the media really wants**

Traditionally, PR concerns itself solely with media relations – the placement of editorial in the media. Practitioners have typically measured their success by the column inches of space garnered in the media.

Editorial space is not for sale at any price. It is space earned by offering the media newsworthy and objectively-written materials. Newsworthy means a product or service that is genuinely new, not a name change or addition to an existing line. It means a product or service that has marketplace distinction or is unique in some way.

All PR writing should be in the third person objective voice, like a newspaper article. It should be specific and concrete. Sales boasts and advertising claims are not what the media wants, nor needs. Strike out unqualified claims, superfluous adjectives, glittering generalities and any sales talk. When a distinguishing claim is made, make sure to qualify it by stating that it is "designed to" accomplish such and such or it is "engineered to" do such and that. By adding the qualifying language you can retain an objective position. Otherwise, the skeptical reader (which includes most good editors) will say: "Oh yeah? Prove it!"

There are many benefits of abiding by the rule of objective writing. First, it shows you are credible, and thus, worth taking seriously. All professional PR practitioners understand that the only thing they can offer an editor is their credibility. If that trust is violated, it will take a long time to rebuild. In some cases, the communication bridge has been burned and can never be rebuilt.

When I was younger, a gnarly old PR practitioner showed me a well-worn brown leather personal address book. This little book, he told me, contained the names and phone numbers of all the editors he has personally worked with. "These folks trust me and I will never, ever do anything to violate that trust," he sad, "Any of them know that if I come to them with an 'exclusive story' that it will be worth their while and that no other publication will scoop them before it is published or eclipse them after it is published." He shared this with me in such an ominous, dead-serious manner that I have tried to build similar relationships with the media over the years. I saw my old colleague's special address book only once, but I have no doubt that he still uses it and will die with it safely tucked in his shirt pocket.

# Jeff Winke

## How to avoid the wastebasket

A second reason for providing objectively-written copy is that it makes it easier for editors to use. If an editor can use your material with little or no editing, it has a much greater chance of being used.

At one point in my career, I was an assistant editor to two trade magazines for the commercial building operations and maintenance areas. As the junior editor, my principle responsibility was to comb through literally 150 or more new product press releases that came in each month and select about 20 of them for publication.

If the task were to merely choose the releases and run them verbatim, it would have been a snap. Unfortunately, most new product releases require editing and rewriting. I remember receiving press releases handwritten on lined notebook paper and releases that were exquisitely printed on cotton bond. No matter the presentation, I soon learned which companies I could rely on for providing objectively-written, minimal-editing releases. Quite simply, these companies received more coverage because their copy was easy to work with.

On the other hand, releases filled with "the best ever," "guaranteed to save money," and other grand claims received my best hook shot in the trash basket. Sadly, some of the most prodigious producers of useless press releases were PR and ad agencies that you would think would know better.

**Becoming a credible player**

When your company is visible in the editorial sections of trade publications, newspapers, websites and magazines, it enhances your company's reputation. The coverage indicates that your company not only exists, but is a player. At a minimum it sets the stage for maintaining existing business and creating awareness necessary for capturing new business.

Armed with this quick overview of public relations, we are ready to launch into the guts of the *PR Idea Book: 50 proven tools that really work.*

This book is an idea source. Consider it a first step for conducting your own internal brainstorming. Take the tactics in this book and make them your own. Manipulate, adjust and transform them into actions that will work for you and your organization.

To make things easy for reference and referral, the tools are ordered alphabetically. Go ahead and jump in wherever your fancy strikes you. It's your sourcebook so read them in any order that you like.

# 1
## Activity Updates

**O**nce a quarter, especially if you are in a dynamic growth mode, forward a summary of the activities your company has accomplished or is currently engaged in to the media. If your company is less active, an annual or twice a year report is sufficient.

The updates serve as a snapshot of the past quarter's accomplishments. In a sense, they become an ongoing archive of releases sent, trade shows attended, stories published, business developments such as acquisitions and expansions, personnel changes, newly published literature, new website enhancements, realignments or leadership changes, and any advisories or information passed on to the editors.

Activity updates can also serve as an alert to upcoming product or service introductions and impending developments of interest to the media. In a sense, it positions the company with the media for the future.

Go ahead and send your activity update as a paper report, but it is probably best suited as an email. The appearance of the email update should be plain and simple, but professional looking. Save the graphic zing for promotional e-newsletters that go to your customers. Editors don't want to feel as though they are being sold to.

Make sure to receive editors' permission to receive your email activity updates. To get permission, you can either survey the editors en masse or collect their O.K. responses during regular contact with them. Make sure to note in your media database which editors have and have not given permission. Of course, you'll want to include an opt-out notice in your emails, so that those who wish to stop receiving your emails will have a mechanism for alerting you to discontinue the flow.

Taking the idea one step further, store the reports online in an activity blog. Blogs are online journals that individuals keep, but the concept is expanding beyond the teenager hoping to share plights, insights and distraught personal episodes with the rest of the world. A company blog can be created on your own corporate website or literally take advantage of one of the free or low cost blog services found online. The reason for maintaining the history is to provide the media with yet another research source when pulling material together for articles. Include links to online press releases, photos, brochures, spec sheets and video snips that can be embedded in the email report and historic blog record.

Pass the same activity update along to other audiences with appropriate cover letters. Employees and the sales network will feel as though they are being kept in the loop. Investors will feel as though their investment is wise. Fellow business leaders in your community and local politicians will be able to brag about your company, feeling as though they have inside information.

# 2
# Advertorials

**P**aid advertising that adopts the look and form of editorial coverage is called an advertorial. Even though this is a paid advertisement, it falls into the category of public relations because the information presented is objectively written.

The advantage of an advertorial is that since you are paying for it, the copy reads exactly as you want it to and you can place the same advertorial in competing publications. Some companies try to make the advertorial look as though it is a part of the magazine's regular coverage, so it is designed with the same typeface, headlines and column width. Magazines will label these "wanna-bes" as "paid advertising" right at the top of the page. The careful reader will notice that it is a paid ad, while many readers will not and assume that the advertorial is part of the regular coverage.

Rather than trying to blend into the magazine's content for the issue, some companies use the advertorial approach to inform and educate. I've seen some very effective "pullout" advertorials that are sequenced in subsequent issues as a building resource that the magazine readers are urged to keep for on-going use. The pullout may be three-hole punched or marked for punching to reinforce the implied message: "Keep this important information handy for future reference."

Some smart ways to use advertorials include:
- Creating a reference-style selection guide that describes the best use of each available model from your extensive product line.
- Developing maintenance tutorials, being careful to describe appropriate maintenance for the product category, but of course using photos of your equipment as examples.
- Positioning your company as the industry leader by publishing white papers or opinions on industry issues.
- Publishing application stories that for whatever reason may not fit the magazine's editorial policy.

These application "features" are especially effective if the advertorial tells part of the story as a teaser. To read the remainder of the story, the reader must either complete the magazine's inquiry card, call your toll-free number to request the full story (that can be emailed as a pdf or sent as a paper reprint) or visit the company's website.

It also is smart to produce extra copies of advertorials, which can be distributed to key audiences important to your business, such as employees, investors and the media. Make certain to include an appropriate FYI message, so recipients understand why they are receiving it.

# 3
# Application Reports

Company paid and produced application reports typically are one- to four-page printed bulletins. They document the problem-solving capabilities of a product or service used at a customer site.

Typically they are arranged with categories in a Problem (or Challenge), Solution, Results, Technical Data format. These pieces tend to be briefer, more direct and to the point than a case history article written for a trade or news publication. Application reports work tremendously well as sales tools. They are most effective as part of a series, since the salesperson then has an arsenal of successful applications to draw from, depending upon the prospect and selling need. Application reports are especially effective, useful, and inexpensive for products sold to a number of vertical markets, where targeted marketing programs can get costly.

Benefits:
- Can be produced quickly, unlike a case history story, which may not appear in a magazine for months.
- May not require the depth of research needed for a feature article.
- Can be produced without naming the customer, since the emphasis is on the application.
- Can work like a customer testimonial when the customer is named.
- Can be used as a sales tool.
- Can educate salespeople on new or unique applications.
- Helps inexperienced salespeople look smart, since they can walk through an application report with a customer.
- Can be used in targeted direct mail to alert prospects with similar applications.

Use application reports strategically. If increased productivity or lower maintenance costs or faster response time are competitive advantages for your company then go ahead and skew your application reports to emphasize your greatest strength. As long as you do not distort or lie, the application report format lends itself to highlighting your strengths.

Additionally, send each application report to the media with a new literature press release to maximize their exposure. Magazines and websites that publish new literature will often run a brief notice. More frequently than you might guess, editors will call to inquire about the availability of a longer version of the application report to run as a case history in their magazines. At a minimum, sending a copy of the application report with a new literature press release provides another legitimate and newsworthy contact with the editors you hope to reach.

# 4
## Article Reprints

**B**y all means, reproduce every published article about your company. Printed article reprints are great giveaways, trade show handouts, direct mailers, and sales call leave behinds.

First, contact the publication and request permission to reprint the article. They will generally grant the request with the requirement that a "Reprinted from…" notice be placed on the reprint. You will gladly comply since that is the whole point: the article about your company or product has appeared in a publication that everyone respects. Most publications have reprint services that will produce quantities of the article for a reasonable fee.

If you decide to reproduce the article yourself, you may want to add a cover or overleaf to the reprint to summarize what the article is about. For example, a three-page article had been placed in a major construction trade magazine for the heavy equipment manufacturer Komatsu, who was a client of the ad agency for which I was working. The front cover of the four-page reprint contained the article's headline, "Making Quality Routine." Below the title, we included an explanatory sub-head: "Komatsu vice president explains the company's new approach to total quality." Taken together, the article title and the subhead, did a good job of explaining what the story is about and the reprint aptly supported the company's marketing and sales push on product quality.

Some companies create a common masthead under which reprints are reprinted in order to tie them together in a common look. When I was working with Harnischfeger, the large overhead crane and hoist manufacturer, we created an "In-the-News" banner that ran above the article headline and a box with a bold "Reprinted from:" header that indicated the magazine name, month and year of publication, and color mini-version of the magazine cover. Every reprint followed the same design so we were able to produce a series with a common look, even though the articles came from different magazines.

The important thing is to not assume that all your customers and prospects will read the article in the magazine. People get busy and may not read that particular issue or, for that matter, they may not get the publication.

Isolating the article from the magazine through a printed reprint is a way of drawing attention to the article and saying, "Hey, this is important and worth reading!"

Article reprints do not always have to be on paper. Don't overlook an emailable pdf and posting the article on your company website. Again, a preview summary or explanatory label will help.

How to use reprints...
- "Door openers" or "leave behinds" for your salesforce.
- Mounted on display boards for distributors to hang up.
- Used with a pitch letter in a targeted direct mail campaign to reach customers with similar needs.
- Handouts at trade shows – particularly industry-specific and regional trade shows.
- Used with product literature to fulfill advertising and public relations spawned inquiries.
- Distributed internally to all employees so they can

see how their product benefits customers.
- Posted on employee bulletin boards to instill a sense of pride.
- Sent to local business press with a FYI-note. The correspondence should be followed up with a phone call to see if there is interest in writing an article about your company, its products/services or its success in the marketplace.
- Training aids for educational purposes.
- Follow-up to prospect inquiries.

A note of caution: Be careful about running off quantities of copies on your company photocopier without getting publisher permission. Whether photocopied or professionally printed, reproducing copies without the publisher's O.K. will violate copyright laws.

# 5
# Breakthrough New Product / Service Announcement

O.K., let's say you truly have an incredible, superlative, better-than-the-wheel, innovative new product or service to introduce to the market. This is the time to think big...really big.

First, consider how big will the tremor be? If it will be felt in your marketplace, that's big. If it will reach beyond your market niche into the business world at large, that's really, really big. Make sure to do a reality check – that is, consult with others outside your organization to confirm that your new introduction is truly a breakthrough.

Assemble an "announcement SWAT team." Include key members of senior management, the technical or idea developers, and sales / marketing / public relations people. Agree on the limits of what can be shared with the outside world before privy and competitive insights are revealed.

Once you've determined the viability of your spectacular introduction, you'll want a press kit with appropriate components. Offer the editors from the leading trade magazines first dibs on the story. You may need to visit their offices if it's difficult for them to come to you. Have them sign confidentially agreements to bind them until a predetermined date. Giving your industry's trade press first crack on the announcement shows respect and honor for your market. It's like telling dear ol' mom that you're expecting a baby before blathering it to everyone, including your nosey neighbor.

Plan the announcement carefully and strategically. Include everything for a complete understanding of your new product or service and its significant impact. If a product demonstration is in order, do it. If a trusted customer has been beta-testing the product, have him or her there (or a video conference call connection). If independent testing was done, have the results and the researcher available. Build in sufficient "wow," but don't go overboard (skip the drum roll and parting floor-to-ceiling velvet curtains).

Significant new product or service introductions are a rarity. Therefore, if you have one, take advantage of the unique opportunity.

Side note: Make sure to document the new introduction and place it in a corporate milestones file. Significant new product or service introductions are important and contribute to your company history – thus, there's value in having a complete record.

# 6
## Business Letter

**W**ithin this digitized, interactive, wireless morass, sometimes the most effective tool is what is becoming today the least likely. A good old-fashioned business letter lends a sense of formality and seriousness to a new product or service announcement, a business development or industry shift. In sending the letter to the media, address it to the managing editor or editor and cc: the publisher and your sales rep for the publication.

Send it in a #10-size business envelope and run the envelope through your computer printer. Don't use mailing labels, since you don't want a mass mailing impression. Use this technique frugally. Save it for the invitation to the big press event or to give the editor information of value – the results of a major company-sponsored study, announcing an acquisition or merger, the availability of a new white paper, or reporting a new design patent.

A client of mine, Electromotive Systems, used this technique quite effectively a number of years ago to announce a major restructuring of its business into two divisions, while at the same time the introduction of a new company logo and corporate graphic identity. The two pieces of information, when combined, made a nice announcement package. If we had tried to make a big deal of either of these developments separately, it wouldn't have had the same impact.

# 7
# Case History/Application Story

Success stories, where your company and its products, services and/or personnel help a customer be more productive or profitable, are great to share with the media. Some editors prefer to write these stories themselves. Others, more often than not, because they are understaffed, like to receive a professionally-written draft that they can edit to their style.

Either a full-length feature or a brief sidebar article can be pursued depending upon the depth of information you have available or to satisfy the trade magazine's editorial needs. Focus the article on the successful use of your product or services, rather than a promotional description of the product or service. Emphasize documented results such as cost and/or time savings, improved productivity, and/or quality, safety or energy improvements. The article might highlight a unique application or a good example of a retrofit. Maintenance or service success can also make for a strong story.

Case history articles are consistently well read. Readers like to see how others address common, as well as uncommon, challenges in their market. They create more impact and visibility than a product announcement does. Because case histories permit an in-depth review of how one customer increased productivity or solved a problem using your product, they resonate in prospective customers facing similar situations.

Both horizontal and vertical market trade publications have ongoing needs for case histories. The story can be repackaged and submitted to other publications. However, it is a big no-no to offer the same story, in any version, to a magazine that competes against the publication that has accepted your article. When I handled Rexnord's conveyor chain division, I'd offer an application story to a material handling magazine and if the story was about a brewery's can-filling line I'd pitch the same story to a beverage industry trade magazine. Further, if the location was a regional production facility I'd contact a local business publication. In this example, my client gets three publication credits for the same story and would have a portfolio of three different stories to use in other sales and marketing efforts.

# 8
## Cause Related Promotions

Depending on the market niche, there might be safety, environmental or community causes that your company could benefit by supporting. Select a cause that isn't politically charged, since you don't want to turn off any of your customers or prospects. By supporting or spearheading efforts on behalf of a beneficial cause, it portrays your company as a leader and good corporate citizen.

It makes sense to choose causes where your products or services are used. For example, if your company manufacturers products that go into residences, then supporting Habitat for Humanity or similar programs with products and monetary donations would make sense. Or maybe, provide support for a local homeless shelter or halfway house.

You certainly will want to promote your involvement with a cause, but before press releases and customer letters are distributed you will want to get the clearance and support of the beneficiaries of your generosity. Clearly, the approach should be that you are proud of your donations and want others to know about them with the hope that your generosity will encourage others to do the same. You also want to make sure your announcements are sensitively worded. With customer letters, you'll want to spread the credit for the goodwill to them as well; by phrasing the letter in away that makes it clear that their business has made it possible for your company to contribute to the community.

Make sure that employees, investors, business associates, and of course, the local media hears about the company's generosity.

Supporting good causes not only makes good PR sense, but it is the right thing to do.

# 9
## CD Press Kit

Including a CD containing the press kit's contents is becoming standard in most markets. It makes sense, since it saves time for the editor and the publication's production staff. Written material is provided in a word processing file and the accompanying photos are provided in print-quality resolution. The CD is typically tucked in the pocket of the press kit folder.

However, most companies do not take full advantage of the CD format's full capabilities. In certain instances, a CD may be a viable alternative to the traditional paper in a folder press kit. CD press kits are advantageous when video or motion graphics would help inform the media. Any time "showing" would be more powerful and informative than "telling," a CD press kit should be used.

A number of years ago, my client Invensys, a large holding company, was attending a major trade show. They had more than 30 press releases that, as paper and attached photos, would have created a cumbersome package, and they also wanted to introduce and explain their new corporate name. Add to that, Invensys executives made it clear that they wanted to portray the company as being technologically advanced. The solution: We put all the releases, photos, and a video snippet that efficiently and effectively showed how the Invensys name came about and what it means onto a self-launching CD with a website-style menu and navigation capability. The Invensys CD press kit accomplished everything the company needed.

A CD opens up possibilities. How about including a photo library of images that an editor can use in the future? What about including a brief video introduction from your company president or founder? What about a snippet showing your product being used with a voice over explanation? Or perhaps an animated technical illustration that portrays a design advantage? A CD can hold a lot of information, so there is much more that can be offered the media in a CD press kit. The key is to make sure that it is organized in an easy-to-use format. It also makes sense to include a table of contents on the jewel case, CD sleeve, or label so that editors can see what's there without having to launch the CD in their computers.

# 10
## Clipping/Monitoring Reports

As media coverage starts to accumulate, it makes sense to monitor and document the coverage your company is receiving. There are two ways to monitor media coverage:

1. Do it yourself by skimming the publications in your market each month for coverage or
2. Contract with a media monitoring or clipping service, such as BurrellesLuce Media Monitoring, PR Newswire or Bacon's Information to "clip" the articles where your company name or products are mentioned.

In the old days, clipping services would provide a pile of articles and mentions cut out from the pages of the magazines and newspapers you had identified as ones to watch. You still can have them provide the actual clips, but most offer electronic clips and nifty electronic clip books. The electronic format makes for email-ready internal distribution.

Although sifting through the published clippings each month, provides one measure of your public relations success, the real product you are receiving is information. The building collection of media mentions and clips provide information that can help you correct mistakes, build on successes, and guide your future actions in the marketplace.

The information can:
- Measure the editorial acceptance of your public relations and news releases – regionally, nationally and even around the world.
- Compile case histories of your products in use.
- Assemble visual aids for business presentations.
- Collect information for marketing studies.
- Help you measure the editorial impact and acceptance of your public relations efforts.

An up-to-date three-ring clip binder can be kept in your company lobby and employee break room to show that your company is active in its market.

To be extra savvy, make sure to monitor internet-based publications, zines, message boards and talk rooms. You can monitor your arch-competitors as well to follow both their editorial coverage and advertising placements. You can compile information for market research and follow industry trends and current issues, as well.

# 11
## Community Relations

To heighten awareness of your company's presence in the communities where your facilities are located, there is no better method than to create a community relations program. Its purpose: To formalize, document and promote worthwhile activities in the community.

Community relations encompasses a lot. It includes everything from the maintenance and care of the company buildings and grounds to very elaborate company sponsorships of events such as holiday parades and firework displays.

The company that funds the building of a city park pavilion or a community health facility is being a strong corporate citizen. Community relations programs benefit the community and bolsters employee morale and pride by contributing to the quality of life. It also sends a positive message to top talent that you hope to attract to your fold.

Crucial in areas where a company might be a major employer or is viewed as a corporate leader, a community relations program may actually be a necessity. Not all community relations activities need to be grand in scope. Simple gestures, such as purchasing an ad in the local high school's yearbook or offering a couple of web pages attached to the company website to be used by a local nonprofit or charitable organization, can have tremendous impact.

Organizations that foster a strong community relations effort can see significant pay off in positive media coverage. Alert the media when actions or activities take place, but don't be disappointed if everything your company does is not covered. With everything, a newsworthy and unique twist helps.

# 12
## Company Backgrounder

An objectively-written description of the company, it's divisions, products, services, key management personnel, position in the market, and vision for the future, the company backgrounder is essential for establishing media rapport. It is a key component in a press kit and is a reference tool that is filed in an editor's active resource files. It indicates that your company is professional and serious about working with the media.

To the unknowing, a company backgrounder may seem similar to a company capabilities brochure. However, a defining difference is that a backgrounder has a journalistic tone and therefore is free of a sales or promotional language. Theoretically, an editor might literally pull information verbatim from your company backgrounder when writing a story that calls for information about your company. Also, unlike a brochure, a backgrounder appears on plain white paper – no photos, fancy graphics, or spiffy type.

A backgrounder is not a brief outline or a fact sheet, it is a fairly in-depth profile of the company. In length, they range from eight to 10 pages for a fairly young company to 30 to 50 pages for a large, complex company.

Backgrounders are "living" documents, which means they should be changed and adjusted as new developments occur. That's why there is always a date on the cover page. The smart editors will call to verify that the information they have is the latest.

A variation of this tool is a Division Backgrounder that highlights the same topic areas of a company backgrounder but is developed for an individual division of a large company.

A company backgrounder is developed for the media, but can be used with investors or for briefing new managers or members of your board. It is a workhorse document with many potential uses.

# 13
## Company Expert Interviews

Q&A-style interviews can be conducted with experts in your company. The company expert Interviews can be pitched to the trade magazines as complete interviews or as a resource for quotes that can be incorporated into other articles. It seems as though every company has the brilliant design engineer or innovator who, if left alone with the wrong inquisitive person, would excitedly reveal confidentialities that your competition would love to know. By conducting the interview yourself, you are able to control how much information is revealed while providing your company Einstein with well-deserved recognition and notoriety.

The interview need not be any longer than six to 10 questions. The questions should focus on ideas, challenges, and dreams for the future. I enjoy asking creative design engineers: "If you were writing a science fiction novel about our industry, what products, which are currently out of our grasp, could you imagine being in use in the future?" Even if the responses are far-fetched, they still will show your company as being visionary and excited about the possibilities the future holds.

To be strategic, it helps to look ahead in the editorial calendars to see what topics will be covered in a few months. Your interview could tackle the topic and once completed could be offered to the editor as a possible, appropriate sidebar to the main article.

If you find the media has no interest in the expert interview, you can print it up yourself for sales handouts, trade show giveaways or for posting on your company website.

# 14
## Company History

**H**istory starts from the first day the doors opened until right now. Reaching a $50^{th}$ or $100^{th}$ year in business is noteworthy. But, there can be plenty of historical milestones before that. Installing your $10^{th}$ system or making your $1,000^{th}$ sale could be significant depending upon your market.

I can imagine a company celebrating its fifth year in business, creating a brief history of its company and accomplishments to date. Why, you might ask, would they want to do that? Quite simply, to remind the media, investors, vendors, employees and others that they are no longer a start-up company. Any company today that reaches the five-year mark has cause to celebrate and boast.

Company histories take all shapes and forms. There are impressive hardbound books, graphically-rich slim booklets, video/DVDs, CD-Roms, high-end PowerPoints, or special websites. The tone can be light and airy to scholarly. The resulting historical document can be used with special customer programs, company positioning, and/or media relations. A company timeline should be incorporated in the company history to provide an at-a-glance overview of the company's growth and development.

By its nature, a company history documents the past. However, there should be forward-looking elements built into the story of your past and the final chapter should be your vision for the future. You want readers to leave your history story with the feeling that your company is strong, stable and using its innovations from the past as the foundation for creating spectacular products and services of today and for the future.

You can make a company history look vital and relevant today by placing call-out bubbles or sidebars throughout that point out how your industry first, patent, or innovation is contributing or affecting your company's product designs or service offerings today.

Years ago when I was working for Snap-on Tools, the large hand-tool and diagnostic equipment manufacturer, I wrote their corporate history. The graphically-compelling booklet was paired up with Snap-on's annual report that year. They were both given to investors in a nice two-pocket folder – history on one side, annual report in the opposite pocket. The covers made the presentation memorable. The corporate history showed a period-looking mechanic proudly holding one of the very first wrenches that Snap-on made. The annual report cover showed a modern-day technician with an electronic diagnostic unit used in today's highly sophisticated automobiles. The combination of the two booklets portrayed a powerful message: Snap-on was the innovator years ago and today it is the technology leader.

A corporate history can be a guide to business decision-making. Sound far-fetched? In this era of job-hopping, a corporate history provides new employees with a thread of continuity and a context for decision-making. A company history is a story of problems solved. It provides a template for the values that framed the decisions that have been made.

When creating your distribution list for your company history make sure to include retired employees, prospective employees, and civic and political leaders. Also, you'll want to donate copies to the local historical society and the business collection of nearby university libraries.

# 15
## Company Resume

**A** clever way to describe a company or large department within a big organization is to present the information in a resume format. For companies that are service providers, the approach can be a clever way of covering a lot of details. A company involved in human resources, supplemental employment services, insurance companies selling workman's comp, or employment software providers are all ideal, but quite honestly any company could use this as a way of presenting capabilities information.

I used this technique effectively to profile the

Appraisals Department of Mortgage Guaranty Insurance Corporation. The Appraisals Department resume had two intended audiences: (1) internally to define to other departments within the company their scope of the department's responsibilities and (2) select customers who use the Appraisal Department's services. Both audiences received a very clear snapshot summary of how the department works. The beauty of it is that it cost near nothing to produce.

The format looked just like a resume and the subject headers were as follows:

*Purpose* – This is a single sentence statement about why the department exists and its mission.

*Personnel* – With a relatively small department or organization, go ahead and list all members from the administrative assistant to the manager. Name, title, direct line and email address are included. Some companies get nervous about providing an employee listing like this for fear that they are providing their competition with a shopping list. If you treat your employees right, there should be no fear of providing the details.

*Responsibilities* – Just like an individual's professional resume, write these up in the present tense, active voice. Here is your list of company capabilities and services, present them as responsibilities. Somehow the idea of responsibility clearly places the ownership for the product or service offered squarely on the shoulders of the company or department.

*Resources/Reports Available* – With regard to MGIC's Appraisal Department this section clarifies what they produce as part of their responsibilities within the company. What prompted this idea of putting a departmental resume together in the first place was the sense that other departments within the company were confused about what reports they produced. To apply this resume category to another company, the label might become Resources/Services Available. Use this area for describing maintenance and repair services, replacement parts, warranties and guarantees, and other aftermarket help provided to the customer.

*Recent Accomplishments* – Include recent key projects, proactive responses to marketplace developments, new innovations and patents, awards received and even something seemingly mundane as "placed the $100^{th}$ unit" of a product "into operation." It always sounds more positive to say that you placed a product in operation or commissioned a system rather than to say you sold your $100^{th}$ piece, system or product.

*Current/Future Projects* – Instead of talking completely historically, include some insights into what your department or company is working on. Provide enough details to make it worthwhile to read. I'm convinced that it is possible to reveal enough without giving away company secrets. Mentioning future goals or projects – even if they are a bit pie-in-the-sky – provides assurance to your customers that you're thinking about innovations that will benefit them in the future.

# 16
## Count-down Articles

Any story that is based on numbered phases, steps or collected ideas is what I call a count-down article. This is an easy way to present a lot of information in an easily digestible format. This book is in the count-down form, since it has 50 proven tools that really work.

Typical count-down articles will describe things like "the three phases of construction machine control," "the 10 steps toward more profitable business operations," "five features to consider before selecting a production-line vision sensor." Because the format calls for the information to be stripped down to the essentials, it fits the reading preferences of many busy readers.

Consider any process or procedure that supports the selection or use of your company's products or services. These can make for effective count-down articles to pitch to the press or to be self-published for use with your customers. The media likes count-down articles since they make for excellent stand-alone or side-bar articles that can be used in a pinch when they have an editorial hole to fill. Caution: Make sure that articles intended for the media are not saturated with your company name or its branded products and services. They should be objectively written and the descriptions should be generic where possible.

Installation or maintenance recommendations lend themselves to a count-down style article – as do many how-to articles.

# 17
## Create Positive Publicity Opportunities

By shifting the focus away from your company, it will shine back positively.

Consider doing something positive in your community to commemorate your company's anniversary or the retirement of a long-time employee or a corporate milestone. Or better yet, do it for no good reason.

For example, commission a local potter to create a couple dozen coffee mugs to be donated to a local women's shelter, along with a generous supply of coffee, hot chocolate and teas. For a modest amount of money you've supported a local artist and helped out a local social service agency. Or work with a local literacy center to provide gift certificates from a local independent bookstore. The center's tutors can give the certificates to their students. With such a gift you've helped out the literacy center, its tutors and students, plus you support an independent bookstore that is likely struggling against the mega-bookstore chains.

Be creative in your efforts and seek out the under-funded and least appreciated. Think in terms of double impact – an artist or social service agency or start-up company employing disadvantaged employees that can use a boost. Then by all means tell the press and customers what you've done, but do it modestly.

# 18
## Customer Brief

In length, a customer brief is no longer than a couple of paragraphs. It describes how your product, technology, or service is being effectively used by a customer. In a sense, it is a tease to peak interest in your company's problem-solving capabilities. Generally, the brief includes the key customer's name and contact information so the press can go directly to them as a source for an article or broadcast segment. Include them in a press kit and attach them to any press releases that feature products or services that the customer is using. Certainly, you will want to use only your best customers who you are confident will have positive things to say.

In a sense, the customers used in customer briefs function like references and should be treated with the same courtesy. In other words, you'll want to request their permission and you'll want to check in with them periodically to ensure they are still agreeable to be potential contacts.

Customer briefs can be used with the media when an editor asks for customers who use your company's product or service. They can also be used in selling prospects with similar needs. A customer brief is a highly targeted zinger that can have multiple uses. You're only limited by your imagination.

A customer brief is like a puzzle piece. Alone it may not tell the whole story of your company's capabilities, but it can explain an important piece of it.

# 19
## Editor Visits

If you want to have impact on editors, go and visit them in their offices. In my experience, the trade press rarely has companies visit. They are usually tickled and will readily make time for your face-to-face meeting. Of course, you will want to be certain the appointment time you have in mind will work in terms of their publishing cycle.

The purpose of the visit should be your interest in learning how to best work with the publication. It is in the publication's and editors' best interests to know a lot about the markets they serve. That's why they will be interested in meeting with your company and why you should interview them about their understanding of the market. You'll be amazed at how much you'll learn.

In arranging editor visits, there are two options:

1. Plan a formal editorial tour where you and key executives from the company arrange to visit several editorial offices in one or more cities.
2. The other option is to schedule an editor visit in conjunction with routine business travel that may take key people to the city of a publication.

Whether it is a formal editorial tour or a side trip attached to another business trip, you'll want to have a strong agenda for your meeting and an offer of something exclusive to make the visit truly worthwhile for the editors. This may be a disk of photos that no other magazine receives or maybe you commission several technical illustrations for the magazine's use. You can always share a piece of industry research that your company conducted or provide access to a big job or a big customer that could result in an exclusive article. Whatever you decide make certain it will be of value to the magazine.

If handled well, your company will solidify its relationship with the publication and will likely receive more and better coverage in the future.

# 20
## Editorial Calendar Opportunities Matrix

Each year, magazines publish a calendar of the topics they anticipate covering each month. The 12-month calendar typically appears in the publication's media kit – the information advertising buyers use for justifying their expenditures, determining the ad space rates, and choosing the months their ads will appear. Smart ad buyers will want their ads to run in the issues where there will be stories relevant to their customers and market.

The media kit is available from the publication, free of charge and obligation, by simply calling and requesting it.

Most publications also have their media kits posted online on their websites.

The publications' editorial calendars can be invaluable in planning your public relations activities. Developing a month-by-month schedule of opportunities listed in the editorial calendars is essential to taking advantage of publications' editorial needs. Watch for opportunities to submit pertinent product or service press releases that match a publication's special focus or round-up section.

The Editorial Calendar Opportunities Matrix should not only assist you in monitoring and pursing scheduled opportunities, but also for proactively suggesting articles and sidebars that fit the month's theme of a publication. The ECOM can also be used to spot chances to expand a publication's planned editorial coverage. The ability to be proactive, not just reactive, is key to effective ECOM use. Don't wait for opportunities and ideas to surface, create them.

A few notes:
- Plan ahead. Editors generally work two months ahead. So, if you're targeting a publication's August issue, start talking to the publication toward the end of May or even sooner.
- Every publication's editorial calendar has built-in room to accommodate other topics. Therefore, don't be shy about offering an appropriate article

## PR Idea Book

idea when you don't see an exact match to topics covered in the editorial calendar.

- If I'm mailing or emailing material for a specific issue, I try to help the editor by clearly labeling the outside of the envelope or in the subject line: "For the May issue."

# 21
## Event Sponsorships

There are two approaches to event sponsorship. You can create the mega-event or campaign where your company name and the successful event become intertwined. Miller Brewing does this effectively on a number of fronts. Each year Miller sponsors a fundraising bike ride for local arts groups in its hometown of Milwaukee. The groups benefiting range from the Milwaukee Ballet Company to the Walker's Point Center for the Arts, a gallery and children's art education facility located in the predominantly Hispanic area of town. So embedded is the Miller name that it seems unnatural to think of it as anything but the Miller Ride for the Arts.

Clearly, by creating and sponsoring a large event or campaign your company reaps the benefits of the positive exposure. The exposure often carries well beyond the event itself. Months after the Miller Ride, it is not totally uncommon to see people wearing the t-shirt they received when registering to be a participant. The media coverage is tremendous. Of course, it helps to have the benefiting arts groups urging the media to cover the event from which their organization benefits.

The other approach is to sponsor a number of smaller events or programs surrounding a theme. Let's say you want children to be the beneficiaries of your efforts. And let's also say that your program is named Children Are the Future (CAF). With the CAF program, a lot of the little things you might already be doing now have a moniker. The ad you buy in the local high school yearbook and the little league team you outfit in uniforms become part of the CAF program. Once a quarter, you have a reason to send a press release to the local media summarizing your various efforts and you have the opportunity to thank your customers with a letter or email that says something to the effect "because of your business we are succeeding and have the opportunity to invest in the children, who are our future."

The advantage of creating a rubric program is that you can assemble a lot of little activities into a common effort. It also gives you the opportunity to go to the media, your customers and your employees with an occasional progress report. Where it could look silly to go to the media with a press release saying you bought a couple dozen Braille books for the local children's home for the blind, it looks magnanimous when placed in the context of a half-dozen other small efforts that fall into your CAF program.

# 22
# Expert Interview Series

**A**n effective way of establishing your company as an industry leader is to conduct and publish brief interviews with the thought leaders and experts in your market.

When I worked with Verex Assurance, the mortgage insurance provider, we developed an interview series featuring leaders in the financial services market. Sure, a good number of these "experts" were Verex customers, but they did offer perspective and opinions on lending and the economic outlook based on their experience in their markets. The pocket size Q&A style interview was a half-dozen small pages in length. It included an executive bio of the interviewee to establish their credibility and their photo.

These interviews were well received by Verex customers since everyone is interested in what their counter-parts thought about the marketplace. Each interview booklet was also sent to the media, which helped solidify Verex's leadership image. More than one editor asked, "How did you get so-and-so to talk so freely?" It was easy. Everyone is flattered to be considered an expert.

Expert interviews can become a section on your organization's website, but I like printed pieces because they communicate a sense of permanence and seriousness that isn't always apparent online.

# 23
## Expert Visitors

If you have an industry expert, out of town or out of country visitor coming to your town or your company take advantage of the opportunity.

When I was working at a small marketing agency years ago I learned that an owner of a public relations agency headquartered in Kosice, Slovakia was to visit our city as part of a multi-location tour of the United States. The purpose was to learn American principles, techniques and business operating principles. I jumped at the opportunity to offer our assistance.

The first priority was to create a schedule of experiences that would benefit her. At the same time, I saw opportunities to create good will with a couple of key clients, the local business media, one of our U.S. senators, and key business associates. We scheduled visits, hosted a breakfast reception and roundtable meeting at our offices that included management from client and prospect companies, a professor from the local university, and the deputy business editor of the local major daily. Additionally, we gave her a tour of our facility, briefed her on our clients and how we do business, and enjoyed a couple of meals together where we learned about her business success in Slovakia. The end result: we established an international contact, received a favorable write-up in the business press and we produced a four-page report along with the clip from the newspaper, which was distributed, to all of our clients.

If you think about it, you may have industry experts or foreign trading partners visiting you all of the time. Or if you are like the company I was with – too small to have that kind of activity, you can seek it out by opening your doors to those of note who will be visiting your city. The other option is to contact a business professor at a local university or college and invite them to visit with their top students. The same kind of royal treatment can be bestowed on the students and their valuable perspective can be beneficial to you, your customers, the local media and political officials. And who knows, you might be entertaining future valuable employees.

# 24
## Fact Sheet

Fact sheets are handy for a number of purposes. They quickly and directly telegraph a lot of details that may be too cumbersome when detailed in other forms. A fact sheet encapsulates a company's demographics and assets. It is a quick overview and reference for editors.

It may include:
- mission statement
- headquarter's address, phone/fax, website address
- year founded
- officers and titles
- divisions and subsidiaries

- products and/or services offered
- markets served
- number of employees
- sales network used and number of salespersons, manufacturer's reps, distributors and/or dealers
- geographic reach
- square feet of production facilities
- production equipment list

As the list above implies, a fact sheet should be easy to skim. Definitely make use of bullets or other graphic elements to facilitate quick use.

This multi-purpose piece should be dated and brought up to date as needed. Include the company fact sheet in press kits and use it in follow-ups with the media.

# 25
## FAQ

A FAQ or list of Frequently Asked Questions can answer the common questions asked about your company or organization. The FAQ is effective for clarifying any marketplace confusion about the company or it's identity in the marketplace. Use it to describe any alliances, acquisitions and affiliations. Sometimes it can be quite confusing as to who owns who and why certain partnered projects take place. For large companies, separate FAQs can be assembled for corporate and individual divisions. A FAQ can also address confusion over trademarks and product exclusives.

Because the FAQ format implies an educational or informative use, it can also clarify confusing technical terms in your market. It can help the reader understand proper use of terminology.

Remember to keep the wording of answers straightforward and objective. Resist the desire to sell. I've seen slick FAQ brochures created to help sell products and services. In my estimation, very few have been effective, since the line of questions are so obviously leading. To avoid leading questions, recruit the help of a journalist and/or a new customer whose experience of working with your company is still fresh. They can help you craft questions and answers that are objective and useful.

Since FAQs provide information in an easy, accessible format, there are numerous opportunities to distribute them. Certainly, you'll want to stuff a copy in each press kit, post it on your website, and use it in editor follow-ups as part of editor briefings.

# 26
## Guest Opinion Editorial

In a sense, writing a guest opinion editorial piece is courageous. By offering insights, assessments and recommendations, it effectively establishes your company as a leader on important business, industry and/or community issues.

An "in my opinion" piece can be written and submitted to the national business press. Even if it is not published, you can still send it to the trade media, customers, and employees with the disclaimer "Submitted to the *Wall Street Journal*."

The best opinion pieces express positive ideas and sentiments that offer creative solutions in a clear, logical action plan. A powerfully-worded, step-by-step opinion piece can literally help move an industry forward. On the other hand, opinions that are divisive, aggressively controversial, or champion a particular political candidate or view are probably best kept private.

It's critical to have several trusted colleagues review the piece before sending it off to the publication you're targeting. It's better to catch phrasing or wording that could be misinterpreted before it ends up in print.

Guest opinion editorials are also an effective means for establishing a new or key executive, or an industry expert working in your company, as a marketplace spokesperson of note. Care needs to be taken, since the individual represents the company in the eyes of readers.

# 27
## How-to Articles

Take advantage of your specialized problem-solving expertise to help demystify a complexity in your marketplace. Describe in step-by-step detail the recommended actions to be taken.

Just like the sword-swallower or fire-eater disclaimer of "don't attempt without professional guidance" you'll want to insert in your article that expert help is advised for best results. Of course, the smart reader will thank you for that advice and recognize that you're the one to turn to.

Even simple, so-called common sense how-to articles

can find an editorial home. Each winter in the north, we get snow. Without fail, every late autumn, articles appear in the local press on "how to shovel snow." The articles are designed to prevent back injuries and heart attacks. The smart shovel manufacturer could, of course, take advantage of this editorial need and write an article that covers the basics while describing the best shovel design for certain types of snow. Of course, the photos accompanying the article will show their products. This is a simplistic example, but if you can extrapolate to your market there are likely many fundamental challenges that your customers face every day. The key is, if you show the reader how to do it faster, cheaper or easier, it will be of interest to publications looking for good how-to articles.

Editors generally like how-to articles because they are "evergreen," which means the article has no time date stamped on it – it will be fresh today or three months from now. These articles can stand on their own, or be used as sidebars to other longer articles.

# 28
## Inquiry Management

I know this may be getting a little off track from pure public relations, but isn't the point of generating coverage to stir up inquiries? Here's all you need to know about inquiry management: RESPOND IMMEDIATELY. Sounds simple, but you'd be amazed at how many companies fumble here. Elaborate inquiry management systems chug inquiries through multiple hands that by the time the respondent receives anything they've long forgotten what triggered their interest, or worse the inquiries pile up on someone's desk who has been thrown the inquiry fulfillment responsibilities as "something to do as you have time."

Inquiries are golden. They are a step in the right direction to a sale. Even the so-called "lame ones" that will never materialize into a sale can tell you something about how you are perceived in the marketplace. What made that person respond? Were they expecting something else and what made them think your product or service would fulfill their need? So, even these "bad" leads can perhaps help you hone your message or lead you into new markets.

When you respond to an inquiry not only include the product or service brochure that describes the features and benefits but also include a copy of the published release, article or ad that prompted the inquiry. If the inquiry came in over your website, include a link to the page that prompted the interest.

Here's a great idea that I would like to take credit for, but can't. I had requested information from a new product announcement in a trade magazine. Within ten days the information arrived. Then, a month later I received a spec sheet for the product and another note thanking me for my inquiry. Then (hold onto your hats), a full year later I received a letter that said:

*Sometime ago – about a year in fact – we sent you information in response to your inquiry about (the product was named).*

*Because we realize that many construction or "update" projects take longer than expected, this reminder is being sent to you.*

*Please let us know if something more is needed to assist you in your decision. We'd certainly like to know the outcome even if it's been shelved, delayed or whatever.*

Wow! I was so surprised to receive a follow-up a full year later that I called the contact person listed to see whether this approach has been worth the effort and expense. He explained that since purchase decisions are not always made immediately (sound familiar?), following up – even a year later – has made a tremendous difference. He also mentioned that since his competition *appears to have problems just fulfilling their leads at all*, their timed follow-ups have caught the attention of prospects and *resulted in new sales*. He also mentioned that they frequently run their "inquiry database" against their "new customer list" to prevent "irritating and unnecessary follow up."

The lesson is – respond to inquiries quickly and then follow up…even if it's months or a year later.

# 29
# Jargon Glossary

If you're in a marketplace full of jargon and acronyms, you can do the media, your customers and employees a favor by producing a pocket-size printed glossary of terms and also posting it on your website along with an audible pronunciation option for multi-syllabic words that are tongue-twisters.

Don't worry about your "first edition" being 100% complete, since you'll want to include an email address where additional words and terms can be submitted. When you publish the second edition, you'll want to include a thank-you page where you list the names of everyone who submitted additional entries or modifications to existing entries.

You'll want to title your booklet the (Your Company Name) Glossary of Industry Jargon and Technical Terms for the (Whatever) Market" knowing full well that over time, and with acceptance, everyone will refer to it as the (Your Company Name) Glossary. You can always invite a couple of the old time, respected trade magazine editors and industry experts to serve on the Advisory Board where they would make sure your definitions are accurate, complete and worded properly. Having them listed in the front of your booklet adds credibility to your effort.

This jargon glossary idea is fairly easy to execute. It requires a detail-minded person to serve as editor and contact person. There will be production costs involved, but it will be a justified expenditure when you consider it will ensure clear understanding and help prevent embarrassing faux pas. Beside, it will serve as a terrific trade show handout and sales call leave-behind.

# 30
## Management Bios

All key managers need current, brief biographical profiles on file. In two to five paragraphs, the bio establishes their expertise and discusses current major responsibilities, significant accomplishments, relevant education, years of company experience (highlighting significant position changes within the organization), as well as, industry experience. If the manager serves on one or more corporate boards of director, those appointments should be included. Although it may be commendable that a manager serves on the board of a local charity, I'd restrain from including it.

After the bio, include several bulleted topic points falling under the header "Content Expert in:" – assuming the manager welcomes inquiries and invitations to speak on any of those topics.

I've seen some management profiles where the executive includes family details, church affiliations and community involvement. For use with the media, that level of information is unnecessary, and in some cases, it's inappropriate.

Biographical profiles are excellent for including in press kits and for briefing an editor who will be interviewing the executive for a story. They are also helpful when soliciting speaking engagements or appearances on industry educational panels.

.

# 31
## Marketplace Studies

Quantitative or qualitative research conducted among customers or your distributor/dealer network can be a valuable way to document industry trends.

For example, Manpower International conducts a Quarterly Employment Outlook Survey in which all of its branch offices throughout the country are asked to make educated guesses on hiring in the various job markets they serve. The managers base their best expectations on the past quarter's performance and their gut feel, based on their familiarity with the market. Each branch office completes a fill-in-the-blank survey. The results are tallied at Manpower's home office. Localized press releases are sent to every daily newspaper, TV station, and radio station serving the markets where the offices are located. The results from all of their offices are accumulated to create a national snapshot of the expected employment trends for the next quarter.

For maximum impact, Manpower distributes local outlook press releases with the national results, and times them for release within a day of the start of the next quarter.

The beauty of the Manpower survey is that it is referred to as an "outlook." They are not claiming empirical accuracy. It's portrayed as an educated guess based on their intimate familiarity with local hiring needs. Manpower receives a tremendous amount of media play each quarter and is positioned each time as an employment authority.

How can you do something similar? Ask yourself: What slice or corner of the market does your company have keen insights into? Can your company produce a purchasing intention survey or a technology adoption survey? Are there opportunities to partner with an industry trade association or trade magazine to produce a quarterly or semiannual or annual marketplace survey?

Clearly, the promotional advantages of establishing an

**PR Idea Book**

annual or periodic study are tremendous. Work with an experienced researcher or research firm to help create your survey instrument, since you want the wording to be simple, direct and clear

## 32
## Market-Specific PR

Sometimes business opportunities arise in unfamiliar markets. I've worked with a number of clients who dreamily looked at the lawn on the other side of the fence and said: "Geeze, that's green." A cost-effective way to know for sure is to slip a toe under the fence and see if the grass is really as lush as it looks. Similarly, a low-risk way of testing a new, unfamiliar market is to tailor market-specific public relations activities to it. The easiest way is to send out a press release or two to gauge reactions as they are published.

A past client of mine, Alloy Products Corp.

manufacturers steel pressure vessels for the processing industries. Some of their vessels are electropolished to a beautiful reflective and super-clean finish for use in the pharmaceutical industry. A manufacturers rep of theirs recognized a unique potential opportunity. While in college, this rep had worked in the funeral business. (O.K., bear with me, you're having the same reaction that the Alloy Products executives had at first.) He knew from first-hand experience that funeral directors did not have the safest and most efficient way of accumulating, storing, transporting and disposing of body fluids collected during the embalming process. He also realized that a small Alloy Products pressure vessel with an appropriate fitting would be a perfect match for an industry need. The rep's research indicated a market large enough to be seriously considered. He also emphasized that the funeral market is very conservative and cautious about adopting new products.

With all that in mind, I recommended we test the marketplace's receptivity to a reusable stainless steel pressure vessel by sending out a new product press release. With the help of the knowledgeable rep, I wrote a release for a product that the company confirmed could be readily manufactured. I also worked with the editors of the two leading publications serving that market to secure placement of the release. Smartly, the company followed up on every lead they received with a phone call to conduct market research and gauge the receptivity of their entry into this specialty market. For the investment of a single press release, they were able to test a brand new market, conduct market research with potential customers, and make an informed decision on cost of entry vs. future sales.

# 33
## Media Day Event

If your office and production facilities reflect positively on the quality of your company's products and services, and help tell your success story, by all means bring an editor or editor group to your headquarters.

Manufacturing and processing facilities that are tidy, organized, efficiently run and staffed by energetic and articulate workers are a joy to visit. Smart companies realize the positive impact their shop has. At every opportunity, they bring customers in to wow them. In the same vein, it makes sense to bring editors through for the same impact.

A facility tour is a key component of a media day event. But you will need to build in more. A carefully choreographed day includes the facility tour, a briefing on your products and services with special emphasis on any new ones that are being unveiled that day, meetings with key management and technical experts, access to several key customers via a panel Q&A session or video conference link, and product demonstrations. You'll also want some "off-the-clock" time, which might be a nice meal, a tour of an interesting local site, or a round of golf. Discuss your off-the-clock plans with the editors ahead of time so you don't take a vegetarian editor to a steak house or a non-golfer to the links. These relaxed times are when you get to know the editors, solidify your professional relationships, and talk frankly about how to best help them serve their readers.

The media day event is certainly an opportunity for your company to display itself at its best, but it's also a chance to learn from the editor or editors attending. Ask the editors to come prepared to talk about their publication, their perspective on the market, where they see the market going, and, perhaps most interestingly, how they believe the market views your company.

The key to a successful media day event is to treat the editors with respect, while providing a bit of VIP treatment. Additionally, make sure to provide them with a press kit tailored to the day. The press kit should include a company backgrounder, press releases on any new products or services announced that day, a contact sheet with the names and contact information for everyone they've met, and perhaps some professionally shot photos of your facility and its production lines.

Make sure to follow up with the editors a few days after the event to thank them for coming and to answer any additional questions.

# 34
## Media List Development

A thorough and complete media list is essential. It is the vital database that helps you achieve your goals.

Among, the best sources for creating your media list are the *Bacon's Publicity Directories.* They publish a number of directories that include a profile of the media source, contact information for the key editors and reporters, and details on what materials they'll consider for publication. Three directories of interest for creating a pertinent b-to-b media list are the *Newspaper/Magazine Directory, Radio/TV/Cable Directory*, and *Internet Media Directory*.

There are a number of computer software database programs out there for capturing and maintaining the media list you create. In selecting a program there are a few features worth considering. It helps to have a lot of information easily available when talking with an editor. In addition to name, title and contact details, it's nice to have the publication's website address and circulation. It also helps to know what geography the magazine covers, if it's a regional publication, and what trade association it is affiliated with, if it's a captive trade association publication.

I like to maintain a history of contacts with the editor. It makes me look smart to be able to say "Hey, the last time we talked was back in November and I had emailed you a press release about the WTF-15 product, was that helpful?" It's also important to maintain sub-lists within the main database. That way if you wish to target only web-based media, you can sort it accordingly.

Whichever software program works best for you is fine. A media list requires continual maintenance and annual "housekeeping," so a program that is easy to edit is important. Changes will happen. Editors leave and sometimes the publications themselves are bought or move their offices.

In some instances, I've found it helpful to have both a computer database and a printed-out workbook format housed in a tabbed three-ring binder. The tabs represent the sub-categories of the master list.

When developing your media list, think outside your vertical niche. Consider all of those involved in the purchase decision. If your product is an OEM component in a larger machine or system, then the design engineering magazines will be of interest. If your product has multiple industrial uses or is a commodity then the general industrial product tabloids should be included in your contacts. Or maybe your professional service is intended for a specific line function but has tremendous bottom line savings, then make sure to include management and corporate accounting journals. With press release distribution you want to cover a wide arc without going over the boundaries of what will be of interest to the readership. Generally, if 20% or more of the publication's readers will have interest in knowing about your product and service, with an eye toward purchasing it or influencing the purchase of it, then include the publication in your media list.

Also, make sure to include appropriate Internet media, trade associations, business media (national, regional, and local) and regional / local publications for key geographic market areas that are of interest to your business.

If you're uncertain about the relevance of a particular publication, call the editor and ask if the readers are likely to buy your product or services. On the occasions I've had to do that, the editors were very gracious as I sheepishly admitted my lack of familiarity with their publication. One editor remarked, "I'm glad you called and learned that we're not a good match for you rather than sending me a stream of releases I can't use."

## 35
## Newsletter / eNewsletter

Newsletters can be either printed and mailed or emailed as a pdf or a link to a website which hosts the newsletter. Regardless of the approach, here are some general caveats. To be effective, a newsletter should be informative and educational, and objectively written.

The more company promotional information in a newsletter, the less effective it becomes. No one likes to read a "me-me-me" newsletter. It is always best to be restrained in your promotion. You'll gain a stronger allegiance to your newsletter, and therefore to your company. I use the 80/20 rule – 80% informative /

educational to 20% promotional. In the promotional percent, I include any ads you might run in the paper newsletter or a banner ad that might appear in the e-newsletter version. The ads should be clear that they are advertising and not trying to masquerade as editorial. Readers don't like to be fooled or played the fool, so being true to your editorial promise of providing "news you can use" is the best approach.

If you feel compelled to have more promotional flair in your newsletter, make it clear that the newsletter contains "news, insights and perspectives." By admitting that you're offering perspectives, it is clear that the "reporting" will be biased. But be prepared to loose readership, since the newsletter will be viewed more as a direct mail advertisement than a helpful resource.

So when is it best to use a printed and mailed newsletter vs. an emailed newsletter? Here's my take:

<u>Printed Newsletters</u> are best when you have the following:
- More in-depth information – meaning stories that are longer than two or three paragraphs.
- You want the reader to spend some time with the newsletter – meaning more than a glance or a quick one-time read.
- You wish to communicate substance, stability and depth. Holding a printed piece in your hands just

feels more serious and worth lingering over than an electronic piece.
- The stories are "evergreen" – meaning the stories are not time bound and subject to be outdated at the time of publication.

e-Newsletters are best when you have the following:
- Briefer, direct information – meaning stories that do not exceed two or three paragraphs and which take advantage of bulleted listing and other compression devices.
- You have timely information – especially if by communicating it indicates that your company is a leader and at the cutting edge of shaping the market.
- You wish to encourage reader response and interaction. It certainly is easier to click on an email link than to detach, fill in and mail a response postcard.
- You've got a well-developed, dynamic website you want to encourage readers to visit.
- You have snippets of motion graphics or video that can more easily communicate information by showing rather than telling. An e-newsletter that links to a website opens up a whole repertoire of dynamic tools that can enhance your newsletter. Links can be provided to other websites, but the problem is that you may lose your reader who may end up wandering off into cyberspace.
- Low budget – e-newsletters in their simplest form

can be very inexpensive to produce. There will be initial set-up costs, but after that the per-issue cost will decline.

So whom should newsletters go to? Customers and prospects are a given. Other audiences to consider include all of your employees, sales reps, vendors, board of directors, bankers/investors, key business associates, trade group leaders, elected officials, the President of the United States – hold on….yes, I did say the President. When I was working with Verex Assurance Corporation, a major mortgage insurance company at the time, we were producing a customer newsletter that focused on marketplace trends and analysis. The Verex manager insisted that a copy be sent to the President. I honestly thought, "well, it's only the cost of postage so what the heck, let's do it." After months of doing this, a call came from a White House research associate asking permission to quote a section of the newsletter in a resource packet being supplied to the President's speechwriters.

This amazing turn of events gave the manager bragging rights internally, as well as to customers. It also helped justify the importance of the newsletter to senior management. This incident taught me to not rule out so-called wacky ideas and to think well beyond the conventional readership to others that might have an interest in your newsletter. If your company produces scientific instrumentation or leading-edge technology, why not send copies to the top science fiction writers, the leading research scientists at the universities, and the governmental officials most interested in your area. For the cost of a couple dozen extra newsletters, the results could be intriguing and beneficial.

The key benefits of newsletters are that they:
- Maintain "top-of-mind" awareness with customers and prospects.
- Position the company as the leader, expert and best source for problem-solving information and products.
- Solidify existing customer relationships and nurture prospects.
- Support sales efforts and bolster salesforce / employee morale.
- Contribute to the "good of the industry" by educating readers in professional practices and the newest technology.
- Demonstrate commitment to the industry.
- Create familiarity and comfort with the company's expertise and personnel.
- Serve as a vehicle for relaying and/or supplementing industry and trade group news.

Newsletter writing style should be direct and free of ornamentation. Use writing devices which facilitate readership and comprehension such as:
- Bulleted points
- Call outs

- Graphs, charts and other representations
- Summary statements at the beginning of in-depth articles
- Subheads throughout lengthy articles
- Listing sources and websites for in-depth treatment of an issue

Clearly separate your company information on new products and services, new literature and newsworthy developments from other articles. If a page or two is clearly marked as "New from (your company name)," it can still be included in the newsletter while not jeopardizing the credibility of the other articles.

Sometimes an unconventional size or format for a printed newsletter will work best. Not all newsletters need to be file-folder sized. Consider a jumbo postcard size newsletter (8-1/2" by 5-1/2"). If handled well, you'd have room for two or more brief articles. Or if your audience is regularly connected to the Internet, the "newscard" could contain a couple of complete brief articles and the lead of a longer article that requires the reader to "jump" to your website to finish reading the complete article. A variation of this might be a greeting card size and shape newsletter that arrives in an envelope with the table of contents and teaser lead-ins appearing on the envelope. If you wanted to be generous and predispose your recipient to read your newsletter while taking a break, include a candy bar in the envelope with each issue.

# 36
## Online Press Room

If you have a company website, creating an online press room or media center should be doable. Use common sense in the layout and navigation. Editors will come to your online press room for information and photos – usually in haste, because they likely find themselves in a deadline crunch. They'll make repeat visits if the site is easy to use. Resist the temptation to have registration and logon passwords.

The information posted in the online press room should be public information that can be published. You don't want confidential information that could benefit your competitors or others.

Good information for the online press room could include:
- past press releases with accompanying photos
- company backgrounder
- company fact sheet
- high resolution photos that can be downloaded
- list of story ideas where company contacts and support is readily available

If you think it would be handy to have online access for key editors to retrieve exclusive-story information, photos or illustrations you can always include a password protected area that you could call the "wall safe." That way you can tell an editor, "I put three high-res photos in the wall safe located in our online press room. The combination for the lock (the password) is 34-22-15. You can pick them up anytime you want for the next two weeks." I'm not certain why you'd need or want an elaborate system like that, but the option is there.

In essence, the idea of an online press room is to provide quick, easy-to-find and useful information for the media.

# 37
## Press Conferences

In the b-to-b arena, press conferences are frequently held in conjunction with major trade shows to capitalize on the convenience of having the media together at one location. Trade shows are also a convenient occasion for unveiling new products and services.

There are typically three locations for holding a press conference in conjunction with a trade show: (1) a trade show management assigned room (usually near the press room where the media tend to congregate), (2) at the exhibitor's booth, or (3) offsite at a nearby location, such as a nearby hotel meeting room.

A press conference should be a carefully planned and executed event surrounding a significant new product/service introduction or a major announcement. It absolutely should not exceed the promised timeframe, which is normally an hour. The agenda should include new product or service presentations, demonstrations, and access to senior executives in your company and knowledgeable technical staff. A time-conscious facilitator needs to keep the program moving on track.

Little extras that will help the press conference succeed may include recorded music as the editors arrive and leave, a snack table with cold and hot drinks and food items ranging from a light meal to a tray of cookies, a parting "thank you" gift such as a company t-shirt or pen (you can get creative here but not overly expensive), and, of course, a press kit which should include copies of the PowerPoints and other presentation materials. You'll also want to collect business cards from everyone in attendance for post-show thank you notes and follow up.

Coordinating a press conference also involves keen observation. If you notice that an editor asking a manager or technician a lot of good questions, you might ask the editor if an exclusive interview would be something of interest. Of course, with any press interview, it is important to have a have a steady, sober PR professional present to kick the manager or technician in the shins should their comments start to wander into proprietary or controversial topics.

It's absolutely essential that the material presented at the press conference is truly new and newsworthy. Otherwise, you'll dash the trust you've built with the media. It's also important to invite the media well in advance of the press conference date. And remind them a few days before the event. The smart planner will get RSVP-style commitments so that the attending media feel obliged to attend.

Press conferences are an efficient way to reach a lot of media members with strong, positive news about a significant new product, service or company development.

# 38
## Press Kit

Press Kits familiarize the media with the company in either a one-on-one media contact, a press event or at a trade show. They include both company background information and the latest press releases.

Attend any trade show and you'll discover a room for the media to collect press kits from the exhibiting companies. Usually, the press room is off to the side and away from the frantic flow of the trade show exhibit hall. This room is where the media relaxes, organizes their notes, checks in with their offices, and sometimes meet with an exhibitor who is invited in to the room. The room

## Jeff Winke

is off-limits to all but registered media.

In the press room, you'll find a number of long tables with press kits stacked high. The press kits are free to the media. No one is standing beside each kit hawking it. Therefore, it is up to the press kit to attract and hold the attention of the editor strolling by. Press kits range from embossed or gold-stamped high-production two-pocket folders, to simple off-the-shelf school folders with and without stick-on labels, to standard 10" by 12" envelopes to the occasional three-ring binder. Although most of the press kits identify the company on the cover, most fail to identify the company's products or business category. A good number of the folders are standard glossy company literature folders with product photos or company taglines such as "Providing solutions for over 60 years." At one food processing trade show I attended, a company cleverly sealed its press kit contents in one of its heat-and-serve TV-dinner containers without the food, of course.

I've attended trade shows and visited the press rooms to collect press kits across all sorts of industries and have found one commonality: most press kits are embarrassing dismal. Let's review the basics that so many companies forget:
- Press kits are intended for the media.
- The media attends a trade show to focus on what's new.
- There can literally be well over one hundred press

kits to choose from at a typical trade show.
- The already busy media is hyper-busy at a trade show.
- The press kit is expected to contain words and pictures of what is brand, spanking new.
- The press kit is expected to familiarize the media with the company.

This all seems simple, right? Fortunate for you, most companies don't get it. You have the opportunity to do it right and win the respect of the editors and earn space in their publications.

A big mistake that many companies make is that they cram their press kits full of useless information in an attempt to portray that they are a company of substance. They include old press releases and ad slicks and product literature that are not connected to any press releases.

I had an embarrassing experience years ago when I had just joined an ad agency. I was less than a couple of weeks with the agency when I found myself standing at a long table with thirty-five stacks of press releases, glossy photos, product brochures, ad slicks, and a piece I swear was the instructions for assembling a bicycle that was probably being thrown in for good measure. The agency owner's elderly retired parents were there earning "egg money" by scurrying around the table collating the press kits, which I was to be responsible for lugging to the show. After the mom said in a good-natured, but firm voice "come on – don't just stand there – jump in," I found myself a participant to the madness.

Needless to say, it was painful for me to meet with editors and have to plunk down the bulging press kit folder. One editor said to me: "I'm not going to cart this monstrosity back to my office, so you better tell me what the two or three truly new and spectacular products are or this whole thing will end up in the trash." Oh kaaaay.

So, how do you prepare an effective press kit? Here's what I recommend:
- Use a folder that clearly identifies your company, its market, and the product / service niche you serve. Your booth number should either be printed or affixed to the cover via a sticker, so the motivated editor can easily find your company at the show.
- Immediately when you open the press kit or paper clipped to the cover, should be a press kit table of contents. Make sure there are contact names, addresses, phone numbers, email addresses and your company website address visible and apparent. If the press kits are being distributed at a trade show, it doesn't hurt to include a mobile number of a contact at the show.
- Your business card should be inserted in the die-cut slots on the pocket or stapled to the pocket.

- Include only press releases for brand new products being introduced at the show.
- If you are compelled by forces greater than you to include old press releases, limit to one or two and clearly label them something like "Significant product (or service) introduced within the past nine months."
- Go ahead and include product literature that relates to the new products being introduced. Make sure you have new literature press releases written about the pieces, since many publications have a "new literature" section.
- The only other literature you might include would be new selection guide, full product line offering brochures and a company capabilities brochure. These should be paper clipped to the corner-stapled Company Backgrounder. Again, if these are new pieces, include new literature releases with them.
- A Company Backgrounder.
- A CD press kit version.

# 39
## Press Release

All press releases should be objectively written and follow the standard, expected flow and format. Remember most editors and reporters are on tight deadlines and have very little time. Therefore, keep your press releases brief and to the point. Maintain a factual, professional writing style and avoid inappropriate adjectives like "wonderful," "fantastic," "innovative," etc. Here are a number of common types of press releases:

- <u>News Release</u> – Report business changes and other "news" in a news release. These might be mergers, acquisitions or alliances, new contracts, large orders, expansions, or new facilities announcements, research results, distributor or representative agreements, trade show participation, awards or honors, milestones or special events, speaking engagements, community involvement, etc. Make sure, if you're naming customers or new business partners in a news release, that you get proper permission in writing from them ahead of time.

- <u>New Product Release</u> – Announce new product introductions, or products that have been substantially changed, enhanced, or upgraded. The focus should be on the unique or unusual product features or applications. Avoid the "proud parent syndrome" when describing your new product. You may truly believe that your product is unique, incredibly efficient and revolutionary – just as you're convinced that your child is the most talented, smartest, athletic and beautiful kid to grace earth. Do you catch my drift? Stick to objectively-written features and let the reader conclude that the product (and your kid) is special.
- <u>Personnel Release</u> – New employees and employees who have changed positions through either promotion or realignment should be announced in a personnel release. Even though most trade magazines do not have room to run personnel announcements they are still worth sending. They remind editors of your company and show that your organization is growing or adapting

to a dynamic market.
- <u>New Literature Release</u> – Any new printed brochures, catalogs, technical bulletins, application reports, posters, selection charts, and other printed or electronic documents can merit a new literature press release. Ideally a copy of the piece of literature should be attached to the release, since this may spawn interest from editors for photos, illustrations or charts contained in the literature that the editor may wish to use in future articles. If you email your press releases to the media, attach a pdf of the complete brochure and a high-resolution image of the cover, just in case the publication wishes to run the release. Remember that any inquiry about literature that you receive from a published announcement is a request for buying information.
- <u>Photo Caption Release</u> – Submitting to the media that one out-of-a-thousand photo that exquisitely captures a product at work or people at work in manufacturing, testing, assembling or servicing will not only provide another press coverage opportunity but will help editors out immensely. Most trade press editors are desperate for good quality photography. When I was a trade press editor, I can recall the publication art directors regularly snooping around our offices while asking if we had "any descent photos that show such and such." The best photos to send with a photo caption

are vertical in orientation (with the hope that it may be used on the cover of the magazine), showing action (people working with your product or your people performing at their peak – e.g., your sales representative unloading heavy equipment to be used in disaster relief while the smoldering volcano spews dust, ash and smoke in the background). Remember: Anytime people appear in photographs, they must sign a model release. That's their written permission to use their likeness in any kind of promotion, including press releases. That rule especially applies to photos showing your customer or customer's installation. If the photo is truly spectacular, you might consider submitting it to the Associated Press wire service where it will have the chance to run in hundreds of newspapers. Recommendation: When possible, hire professional photographers. The results will be better and contracting pros will help to build a valuable library of quality photographs.

- <u>Press Advisory</u> – A press advisory is an informative notice sent to an editor with the understanding and expectation that it is not intended for publication. It is sent to the editor out of courtesy to keep them up to date. There are many trade publications that will not publish traditional news releases, as described above, but the editor still appreciates hearing about new business developments. A press advisory appears in the same format as a press release but is clearly marked. Editors appreciate the fact that you know the difference between information intended for print versus that being provided to them to keep them up to date.

With press releases in general, I recommend staggering their submission to the media to ensure maximum opportunity for them to be published. For instance, with a monthly publication, sending a new product release every five to six weeks is adequate. An exception to that rule would be special trade show issues, product round-ups and buyer's guide issues. In these cases, the envelope or subject line of the email should read: *For the June Excavator Round-up Section*, so the editor realizes what your intent is. Targeting the release in that manner, shows respect and familiarity with the publication's publishing schedule.

If your company's products are mature and unlikely to be surpassed by any new technology or major modifications, a product release can be recycled every year. The justification is that there are new readers of the publication. I worked with Alloy Products Corporation a manufacturer of ASME-code pressure vessels. Although the pharmaceutical, specialty chemical, and food and dairy processing industries are very dynamic, the pressure vessels are very simple – elegantly simple. To maximize their exposure in the trade press, I repackaged their collection of product press releases each year. By repackaging, what I mean is that the release was modified to emphasize a different feature and a new dramatic or artsy product photo was provided. With this approach, I was able to keep their products in front of their potential buyers and existing customers.

# 40
# Radio Presentations / Interviews

Talk radio programs are always looking for interesting guests and topics. Choose an executive who is articulate and quick on their feet. Make sure your product, service or industry topic can be portrayed with enough general public interest.

Even if the radio show is only a local broadcast, there is value in having your dynamic executive on the program. Why, you ask? Bragging rights. Your employees will enjoy hearing it. If the radio station is web-broadcasted, you can literally alert customers throughout the world to tune in via the Internet. And you can inform the trade press through a press advisory. If the broadcast went well, you can also work with the radio station to obtain a copy for posting on your company website.

However, not all company executives are comfortable speaking to the media. Many stern-chin managers roll their eyes at the mention of media coaching. To them, the idea of practice sessions, designed to make them sound good, can sound…well, quite silly.

Here are a few suggestions for the budding radio personality:
- <u>Never wing it</u>. Being immersed in some subject every day doesn't mean you can spontaneously string together pearls of wisdom.
- <u>Over-prepare the basics</u>. Don't stumble on the simplest questions: What do you do and what does your company do? Have brief, action-packed, pithy responses on the tip of your tongue.
- <u>Set goals for the appearance</u>. What are the two or three objectives you hope to accomplish through the interview? Plan to hammer home some key messages.
- <u>Shape your message</u>. Get out the message you want while still responding to questions and ceding control to the interviewer.
- <u>Nothing is 100% off the record</u>. Anything said casually, in jest, or "just between you and me" off

air can come back to you as an embarrassing on-air question.
- <u>Learn how to "bridge."</u> Deflect any intended or unintentional derailments by creating a transition so that you can move from one subject to the message you want to communicate. Use bridging phrases such as:
    - What's important to remember, however...
    - What that means is...
    - That's a good point, but I think you'd be interested in knowing...
    - Let me put that in perspective...

# 41
## Speaker Program

Having a list of speakers and topics available, is ideal for gaining greater presence at conventions, forums, and industry meetings. The speakers' bureau, as it is referred to, should include those in your company who are effective and comfortable in front of an audience.

You might have strong presenters who do well in small, informal settings but, who freeze up in front of a large group. Go ahead and assemble a list of presenters, indicating suitability for specific venues. Use icons to show their presentation strengths. For instance, a star shows availability for small group presentations while a check mark means they're available for panels and a black triangle means they're available for large group presentations. The speaker with all the icons indicates someone comfortable in all settings. Make sure to include areas of expertise. To make a speakers' bureau manageable, you might develop two or three standard presentations with variations to accommodate different speaking settings. Go ahead and invest some time and energy into creating a PowerPoint presentation, since PowerPoints are typically easy to change and adjust.

Of course anytime someone is scheduled to speak, you'll want to generate a press release announcing it. That same press release can be sent to your key customers with a hand-written note on top that says: "I wanted you to be aware that Mary Malone will be speaking at the Chicago area chapter of the Association for Quality Control about our 'Zero Tolerance for Errors Program.' Enclosed is a copy of the press release we'll be sending to the media next week." By sending it to key customers before releasing it to the media, it sends a message to your customer that they are special and getting "inside" information before any others including the press.

And don't forget the speech itself. Many times it can be repackaged as an expert opinion piece or it may become the foundation for a white paper.

# 42
## Special Events

A special event is just that – something special. Therefore, you don't want to fabricate a special event for the purpose of generating publicity. Certainly, if your company is hosting a visit by the President or honoring an employee who won an Olympic gold medal or even something more modest, but out of the ordinary, you'll want to create a special event out of the occasion.

Unfortunately, not every event is newsworthy. I had a large bank that was going through a tremendous growth spurt. It seemed like every few weeks they were opening a new branch location that involved a grand opening celebration. I was able to get coverage in the suburban weeklies where each branch was located, but my client was getting frustrated with the lack of attention that the large metro daily newspaper had for the clowns, balloons, coffee and cake that he felt made each grand opening exciting and newsworthy. In frustration, he hired an airplane to trail a banner with the grand opening message on it. He insisted I take a photo of the plane up in the sky and to overnight it with the press release to the business editor of the metro daily. He wasn't happy when I told him as tactfully as I could that the photo looked like a fly pulling a fortune-cookie fortune. The truth was that the large daily finds grand openings to be passé.

What I was able to do – to save face and credibility – was to call the business reporter for financial services and to say: "I bet you wonder why you've been receiving all of these press releases for new branch grand openings? I hope they haven't been too much, but I wanted you to get a sense of the tremendous growth my client is experiencing. If you've got a few minutes, I'd like to outline their expansion strategy, the number of new jobs they've created and where they plan to be in six months with hopes that there might be a story angle I could help you with." The strategy worked and the newspaper ran a modest article. I was elated, but my client still didn't understand why the paper wasn't interested in the number of people at the grand openings, the number of new bank accounts opened and the number of children who got their faces painted by the clowns. The lesson to learn is to realize that a terrific and important special event may be special to you, your customers and your employees but, unfortunately, it may be old hat to much of the media.

Special events do not just happen. The planning, arranging and organizing can take months even as much as a year or more in advance to plan. There are tomes written about the logistics involved in special events. I am not going to get into that. What I am interested in is how to make a special event special enough to merit press coverage. This is a toughie. The local media has witnessed every grand opening, anniversary celebration, and honorary roast dinner. The business media doesn't much care unless there's economic impact – meaning jobs gained or lost. And the trade press generally could care less, unless they have an "In the News" section that needs another blurb.

A single news release announcing the pertinent information works well for a simple event, but a large, complex event can justify a series of advance stories or teasers, especially if big-name VIP's will be involved or the event falls into the man-bites-dog unusual news angle. For example, if your company is locating its new manufacturing facility in an economically depressed central city area, rather than in a leafy suburban manufacturing park, your ground breaking ceremony will carry more news value.

In planning a special event, it is crucial to define your purposes. I made "purpose" plural for a reason. Yeah, you might be honoring retirees including Gus who started in the mailroom when he was 15 and has spent 50 years with your company, but the event should inspire and thank all of your other employees and maybe it should thank some of your long-time good customers who made it possible for your company to be successful enough to hold on to Gus for all those years. By reshaping your special event purpose, you not only can create a more significant event, you will, in this example, provide a grander send off for Gus and his fellow new retirees. The larger in scope and more reasons for the event, the greater the chance of hooking the interest of the media.

If the event has only local interest, it still merits an announcement to the entire media list, but I would switch the releases going to the non-local press to press advisories. A press advisory, rather than a press release, is used because you're acknowledging the content is intended as FYI and may not have news value.

# 43
## Standing Paragraphs

These are the concluding paragraphs or "graphs" that appear at the end of all press releases. I include this as separate from the various news releases discussed elsewhere in the book because they are important.

First, but probably of least importance, is that including standing graphs on all of your releases separates you from the amateur. Secondly, they familiarize, educate, and in some cases remind the editor of what your company is about. Standing paragraphs rarely see print. That's not their purpose.

Since standing paragraphs function as a little biography of your organization, they should encapsulate the who-when-where-what-why of your company. Because they are a tiny corporate profile, they come in handy for those occasional requests that may come in the form of "send us a brief description of your company" for our directory or to include in the program to acknowledge your company's generosity or for our listing of fastest growing companies. These types of requests and others can probably be satisfied with passing along the standing paragraphs.

The standing or concluding paragraphs are one to four paragraphs in length that generally include most of the following:
- Year founded
- City and/or address where you are headquartered
- Your company website address
- Major products manufactured and/or services provided.
- Marketplaces served
- Geographic scope in which you operate
- Size and placement in the marketplace

The danger is to assume that "everyone knows us," thus there's no need to include standing graphs on your releases. Wrong. Dead wrong. Editors change. New editors join a magazine and need to learn the market and old time editors can learn a detail that they hadn't previously known.

I can remember being a young buck working as an assistant editor of a trade magazine in a market I was just learning. One of my tasks was to select new products to run in the new product section. I remember having separated the releases that I planned to run from those that were to be dumped when my managing editor plucked a release from the dump pile and said "how come you decided against this one?" My response was, "Well I didn't see much about this product that seemed important." Being the nice guy that he was he said: "You might be right, but this is from the largest manufacturer in the industry so we'll want to make absolutely sure that it's not significant before dumping it." When I asked how to become smarter on the players and the products, he told me to read the standing graphs at the end of the releases. And you know what else he said? I can almost quote him verbatim. He said: "The releases that don't have standing graphs are almost certain from *%bleakin'#! losers." When I flipped to the PR side of the business I made absolutely sure that every release I sent carried concluding paragraphs.

## 44
## Syndicated Column

This tactic is very effective when it's important to reach prospects through regional and/or local newspaper weeklies and some trade magazines. The idea is to write a ready-to-use stream of journalistic articles that publications can use as either filler or in a regular author's column or series of articles. The material is intended to be published simultaneously in a number of newspapers or magazines.

A syndicated column is appealing to an editor if the author is a recognized authority or a clever, insightful essayist. The content should be about issues, ideas and advice, not about products or services your company profits from. For example, the expert from a residential electric circuit box manufacturer will want to write about "How to Assess Whether You're Overloading a Circuit," "Ten Electrical Safety Tips that All Homeowers (and Renters Too) Should Know," "Crucial Questions to Ask an Electrical Contractor Before They Step Foot in Your Home," etc. Syndicated columns are either educational or entertaining in tone, never sales oriented.

The value of a syndicated column can go beyond the publications that run them.

Even if your company's article only appears in the Sister Bay, Wisconsin-published *Peninsula Pulse* and reaches just a few thousand readers, the article can be repackaged as a sales-distributed clipping or as a piece in your company newsletter with a footnote that states this is a nationally syndicated column. Through repackaging and/or reprinting, it is possible to give syndicated columns greater exposure.

# 45
## Technical Articles

Articles that focus on specialized technology can make for compelling reading. Articles that always seem in demand are ones that explain how technically sophisticated products work, troubleshoot common problems or describe maintenance techniques. If your company, for instance, created its market or sliced the niche more narrowly through innovative technology, you've got stories to tell.

A kissing cousin of the pure technology article is the "selection guide" article where you tell the reader about the key selection criteria for choosing the best product or service to fill a marketplace need.

In any technical article, it's best to be restrained in mentioning your company name or branded products and services. In a selection guide article all the criteria for selecting the best product or service will of course reflect what your company can offer. That orientation in the article, when combined with either your name, title and company affiliation as the author of the article or a credit at the end of the article of "Information provided by" will be more powerful than inserting your company name every fourth line throughout the article. Readers like valuable information better than sales messages.

# 46
# Technical Brief / Profile

Focusing on a specialized production process or the advantageous features of a product or specialty service, the technical brief or profile provides more in depth information than a product press release. The difference is that the technical brief / profile focuses on *how* the product or technology works rather than the fact that it exists and is available for purchase.

Any company-produced manuals, technical reference materials, training courses, design engineering proposals, or funding proposals can serve as the source material for developing this generally two- to five-page article.

## Jeff Winke

Technical illustrations, schematics, product cut-aways, or process-flow diagrams are often more appropriate accompaniments than product photography.

When used with the media, the intent is to provide a more in-depth technical write-up on your product or service. Often these write-ups appear as longer or showcase product announcements in a new product section or a relevant product round-up. Sometimes they are used as fractional-page fillers.

A technical brief / profile differs from a white paper, which can be longer and is more issue or trend oriented.

# 47
## Trade Show PR Efforts

Trade shows may be the best opportunity to meet with the key editors in your niche. To take advantage of all the public relations opportunities available to you, develop your strategies across three phases: pre-show activities, at-the-show activities and post-show activities.

*Pre-Show Activities*

Planning and actions should take place months before the trade show. The key trade magazines will carry pre-show coverage. Many carry new product round-ups. You may not wish to steal the thunder from significant new products to be introduced at the show, so the best rule is to supply releases and photos of the most significant recent product or couple of products that you've recently introduced. Make sure that photos are different from what you originally provided the media, so that there is more incentive to run it. Modify the release to reflect the emphasis of the trade show.

When my client Rexnord Corp., who manufactures plastic conveyor belts that they refer to as conveyor chains because they are made with plastic composite links, exhibited at the Baking Industry Exposition, I made sure that releases going to the food, snack and baking trade press emphasized the features, benefits and applications pertinent to commercial baking operations. Certainly the photos accompanying the releases showed crackers, baked snacks, or cookies rather than beverage cans, packaged convenience food, or raw chicken.

I also included at the end of the release a statement that read: Rexnord Corp. will be exhibiting this product and others in Building A, Booth #3014 at the Baking Industry Exposition. Some publications actually ran that plug, but it was included more for the benefit of the editors to cue them to the release's use in the pre-show issue and to subtly encourage them to take note of where Rexnord will be located at the show with hopes that they will be added to the "must see" list.

# PR Idea Book

Additionally, you'll want to learn who is producing the "show daily." The show daily is the newspaper published each day for convention attendees. It covers the news of the previous day and highlights what's on schedule for the day. The show daily is published early in the morning and is often delivered to the conference hotels, stocked on the shuttle busses and is available at the doors to the exhibit floor. Typically, the show daily is published by one of the major trade magazines.

I like to find out who the editor is and will contact them well in advance of the show. I'll make a deal that will go something like this: "I'll give you the exclusive right to receive the press releases and photos of the new products being introduced at the show if you will consider them for the show daily. If you decide not to use them, I want your word that you will delete them from your computer; empty your computer's trash twice; rip out the hard drive; and beat it with a baseball bat." Going over the top in melodrama gets the editor to chuckle, while driving home the point that the releases are not to appear in their mainstream publication or taken lightly. Quite honestly, my objective is to get a nice write-up in the first issue of the show daily. I want to reach the show attendees when they are fresh and eager to explore the show. My hunch, and I could be dead wrong, is that, as the days progress during a trade show run, attendees start to run out of steam and many are overwhelmed with the feeling that the show is so big they'll never see everything they want.

159

Thinking positively, I'll pack a couple of different size display frames where I've pre-printed a header that says "As seen in the ASRAE Show Daily" on the card stock insert. That way I can mount the clipping and display it in the Plexiglas frame on one of the booth counters. If I've guessed wrong, I can still offer the frames to exhibitors who were lucky (hopefully they are a customer or prospect worthy of our generosity).

Certainly, if you have plans to host a press event at the show, the invitation process begins months ahead as well. You will want to talk with the key editors to let them know that an event is being scheduled and to gauge their interest level. I would start these conversations even before you have committed to reserving space and holding an event. If you are a big player in your market, chances are you will be able to write your own ticket in terms of time and place. If your presence in the market is more modest, you'll want to test the water first before hosting an event and being embarrassed by minimal turn out. Even if I am representing the most significant manufacturer in the market, I will contact the key editors with my hat in hand. My telephone conversation goes something like this:

> **Me:** Hi Virginia, I'm calling on behalf of Electromotive Systems. They'll be exhibiting at the upcoming ProMat Show . Are you planning on attending?

**Virginia:** You bet...I wouldn't miss it.

**Me:** Electromotive Systems will be introducing two new significant products at the show, plus senior management will be there to talk about their tremendous growth over the past year and the head of engineering will be available to give insights into what innovations they're working on currently. We're thinking about holding a press conference or a breakfast roundtable meeting with key editors like you. Would either of these be of interest to you?

**Virginia:** It's early yet, so I don't have a clue what my schedule will be. I'm guessing that all the big guys will be holding press conferences that I won't want to miss, so at this point I'd be inclined to want to attend a breakfast meeting before the show floor opens.

**Me:** Thanks for the input...we're still at the planning stage ourselves, but I'll let you know what we decide and will contact you immediately with hopes of getting penned into your schedule. By the way, are you planning on producing a pre-show issue and how can we best help you out with materials?

You'll notice that the conversation was direct and took

but a few minutes. This was done to honor the editor's time. If I sensed that the editor was pressed for time, I wouldn't have added the "by the way" and would have thanked her for her time and input.

The conversation accomplished several things. First, it alerted the editor to the fact that there are new products being introduced at the show that we think are significant enough to merit a press event. Second, we got some evidence that a press conference may have some difficulty competing against the big players. And third, we left the editor with the impression that we are professional and respectful of her time.

Certainly when the nature of the event is decided, I'll give the editor a quick call to claim her time and will follow up with the formal invitation to the event where I'll reiterate the details in either an email or printed invitation.

If it becomes clear that editors will not be inclined to attend a press event – which occurs frequently when the company is new to the market or produces such a specialized product that it's difficult to compete for attention against the bigger products – I'll schedule visits to the booth. I'll explain that the visit will last no longer than 30 minutes and that they will have access to a technical expert who will explain the product's features and benefits.

Whether you hold a press conference, host a breakfast roundtable meeting or schedule individual editor tours of your booth you will want to provide each editor with a press kit and a thank you goody. The goody should be something nice and useful – and typically it will carry your company name or logo to act as reminder to the editor. Caterpillar frequently gives editors a scale model toy of one of its pieces of heavy equipment. These are quality, collector-style, metal toys not plastic discount-store specials. The toys are coveted and typically displayed on the editor's desk or bookcase. These little pieces of "yellow iron" provide a terrific reminder of Caterpillar. Certainly you don't want the editor goody to be too expensive to look like a bribe but you want it to be more than a 79 cent plastic pen. My recommendation is to select something that gives the recipient a bit of a flutter in the gut…a "gee, that's nice." It's a fine line, but you clearly want to fall well between a "what a hunk of crap" and a "wow! this is incredible!" reaction. The intent of the goody is to serve as an adequate thank you and hopefully have lingering use or value that it will serve as a positive reminder of your company.

*At-the-Show Activities*

Certainly, your first priority is to ensure the success of any press event you are hosting. This includes checking and rechecking with the facility to make certain everything is in order – even if you had confirmed everything the day before.

Make sure you come to the facility with contact names and numbers in hand. I use the plural of both of those for good reason. You want your main contact and their back up's name, office number, cell number and pager number so that, if things are not set up as agreed within 20-30 minutes of your event start time, you will have a way of contacting them. If everything is up to snuff, you'll want the contact numbers so that you can call to profusely thank them for all their hard work in getting things arranged. It is not only a nice and courteous thing to do, but often the contact person will swing by to find out if you need anything else. They are usually so shocked at receiving a compliment that they'll bend over backwards to make sure everything goes off as planned.

In addition to coordinating any event you host, there are other actions you should engage in. For the public relations professional, a trade show is a bit like being a kid in a candy store. The opportunities to meet with editors are there for the taking. You should come equipped with a "hit list" of editors that you wish to meet. Compare the list of attendees at your event to your hit list and seek out the ones who missed the event.

Trade shows typically have a press room which is where editors go to relax, review their notes, and even write a story or two. The press room is where press kits are placed so editors can collect them. And the press room also has a message board or mailboxes for leaving notes for specific editors. On a plain notecard, of which I carry a supply with me, I'll jot a note something like this:

Hi Joe –

I'm hoping you might have 15 –20 minutes of time where I can catch up with you regarding my client Honeywell Micro-Switch. We can meet here in the press room or I'd be happy to buy you a coffee or beer wherever it's convenient. I want to point out a couple things in the press kit, plus I've got a couple of story ideas that may be of interest to you.

Call my cell phone 414-555-1212 or leave a message on the message board for me as to how best to find you.

Jeff Winke
PR Counsel for Honeywell Micro-Switch

I use my same stash of notecards at the booths of publications that are exhibiting at the show. For editors in attendance at the show I'll leave a similar note as the one above if the editor happens to be out visiting booths or attending press events. For the assistant editor who was not deemed important enough to bring to the show, I'll sweet talk someone into hand carrying a note back to them. In the note I'll say something like "I understand you were left in charge of the magazine while others were at the show. I'm sorry I didn't have a chance to meet you. Hopefully I'll have the opportunity in the future." I do this bit of nicety for two reasons: one, I was once a "lowly assistant editor" so I have a special empathy and, two, I know that today's assistant editor may become tomorrow's managing editor, so it doesn't hurt to plant a few acorns with the expectation that some will turn into oaks.

Other booths worth visiting and leaving a press kit behind include any trade associations and colleges and universities that are exhibiting. The expectation is that the trade association leadership and a professor or two at the college may find the material helpful. It may be a long shot, but you never know what customers or media they might know. I'd rather have them familiar with my client's products than the competitor's. An investment of a few press kits seems like a small price for potential benefit.

As you meet with editors, you will want to take notes. The act of taking notes not only indicates to the editor that you're interested and serious about your professional relationship with them but it will capture important details that you'll use in follow up. I try to capture and organize my notes into three sections:

1. Topics Discussed
2. Opportunities
3. To Do List

It's simple and the information is organized for follow up and future reference. Whether you use a pad of paper, notebook or PDA, it's important to take plenty of notes so that you have a record of what was discussed, what was promised and requests that the editor has made of you.

*Post-Show Activities*

When you pack up and return from a trade show, your work is not done. Wait a few days to allow the editors to resettle into their day-to-day workflow and then begin follow up. Review your notes, collect your thoughts and then plan your call.

Using my notes, I will first review what was discussed and act on the opportunities that we agreed to. I will complete as many items on the To Do list before making my follow up call. Things that usually fall on the To Do list are requests for a particular photo that you have or maybe sending a press kit to another editor with the magzine or maybe getting a technical question answered. I'll also take a look at my ECOM to see what editorial opportunities lay ahead that maybe we did not discuss.

The follow up call will close the loop on your at-show

face-to-face meeting. The call should thank the editor for their time and the opportunity to help. You will want to agree on the specifics and timetable for an editorial you plan to provide. Will you be providing a written draft or information and contacts so they editor can write the story? What photos and/or illustrations will be needed? When does the editor need the materials? By the way, whatever you commit to should be summarized in a brief email so that "you've gone on record." In concluding your telephone call, I'd say something like "I noticed that your issue six months from now has special editorial that we can help you with. I will make note to contact you when you start planning that issue to see if we can help you in any way. Is that O.K. with you?"

The fact of the matter for editors is that a trade show is too big to cover effectively unless they plan ahead. Look at the numbers. Assume there are 500 exhibitors and 250,000 sq ft of floor space, not to mention seminars. If the exhibit space is open for five days, an editor who wanted to talk to every exhibitor, without stopping for lunch or break, would have less than four minutes to spend at each exhibit. And that doesn't account for time spent walking from one exhibit to the next, talking to people they meet, or anything else.

# 48
## Video News Release (VNR)

**H**ighly effective in instances where there is a strong visual component to the press release being sent, a VNR is designed for the TV/cable media, but can be strategically used with the print media.

The aim of a VNR is to capture maximum exposure on television news. In order for a VNR to be effective it must have news value. Effective VNRs offer a news "hook", good visuals, good production standards, timeliness and good coordination. VNRs tend to make more sense for consumer products rather than b-to-b. They are worth considering if your product or service has concentrations of customers in certain locales or you have manufacturing facilities that are significant in a city. A VNR that sees play can create awareness and predisposition to buying among customers and it can provide pride and goodwill among employees, which can be helpful if there's the potential for any worker strife.

VNRs can be either timeless stories that a station might hold as file footage or it may be a story on a breakthrough that has urgency to report. Certainly stories of interest to the general public will get play over a story of limited or targeted interest.

Some standards to follow with VNRs:
- Produce a self-contained package of 90 seconds that can be aired on its own.
- Include an additional two to three minutes of "b-roll" file footage, "sound bites," and additional interviews so the TV producer can repackage the story.
- Provide two "mixed" versions – one with an announcer voice over and the other with what they call "natural sound on tape", in other words without the voice over so that the local TV station can insert their TV personality's voice.
- Make sure the quality is broadcast news-quality footage.
- Never use a stand-up reporter. Stations do not want a reporter appearing on their newscast who is not on their staff.

## PR Idea Book

Always have your announcer sign off with the standard outcue: "This is John Doe reporting."

Before jumping in with both feet producing a VNR, it helps to meet or talk with the news directors of the stations serving your market to ascertain receptivity and preferences.

# 49
# Web Monitoring and Posting

Monitoring the media on the World Wide Web for coverage and mentions can be revealing. "Clips" can be compiled from electronic newspapers and magazines and web-editions of printed publications. Additionally, web user groups, chat rooms, forums, listservs, e-newsetters and blogs can be monitored to keep up to date on the latest dialogue on issues that concern your company. You need to know what is being communicated on the web about your products and your company. Thousands of groups can be monitored daily by using an Internet monitoring service (see Clipping/Monitoring Reports). The information is carefully edited to meet your instructions and emailed to your computer or posted to a password protected web site.

In many cases, there is no reason why you can't be proactive and initiate or jump into existing news groups and forums with your ideas. Again, information providers and problem solvers are appreciated more than those with a sales agenda.

Since the electronic media and postings can be updated or changed with a few computer keystrokes, monitoring must be frequent – daily or even hourly during times of crisis or high marketplace activity. The Internet world is more fluid, quicker paced and dynamic. Sometimes contracting an automated service that can scan hundreds of thousands of traditional print and Web-based articles and postings each day with reports emailed daily can be helpful for catching spikes of unanticipated interest, rumors or controversy before they are out of your control.

# 50
# White Paper

**W**hite papers got their name because they are straight-forward, non-spiffy serious reports printed on plain white paper. They articulate a corporate position on a salient issue or summarize the findings of a research project or offer insights based on the company's involvement in the industry. White Papers position the company as knowledgeable experts in the industry.

They are a type of monograph since they approach the topic with a research and education mentality. The length is determined by how much detail is required to treat the subject thoroughly. Because white papers have substance, they tend to be more than a few pages in length. Most of the ones I have seen and read are 20- to 30-pages long.

The white paper's topic might be immediate and current, but the objective writing should be almost timeless due to the fact that the topic is researched and treated seriously.

# Where Next?

**C**ongratulations on finishing the *PR Idea Book: 50 proven tools that really work*. The nature of this book is to open doors. Some will accurately say, "Hey, you forgot this great idea!" I welcome that kind of thinking. If this book has stimulated analytical thoughts about how best to work with the media and ultimately reach customers with a company's best messages – all the better.

Remember: this book is an idea source. Use it for reference and referral. Pluck it off your shelf when you're faced with creating a gameplan for promoting a new product or service. Use it when devising or revising your company's annual marketing plan. Take the tactics in this book and make them your own. Manipulate, adjust and transform them into actions that will work for you and your organization.

It's up to you to adapt and create solutions that will help push your company and its products and services into a successful future. Go ahead. Do it. I'm confident you can.

Printed in the United States
86718LV00002BA/175/A